The Instructed Conscience

The Instructed Conscience

The Shaping of the
American National Ethic

———

By D. H. Meyer

University of Pennsylvania Press

Philadelphia

BJ
35 2
M49

Text designed by John Anderson

Manufactured in the United States of America

Contents

Illustrations

Introduction

This is a book about books that played a significant role in the formation of America's public conscience. Specifically, it is a study of college texts on moral philosophy written in the United States in the mid-nineteenth century. I first became curious about these now almost-forgotten writings in my effort to gain a clearer understanding of the mainstream of American values and convictions, and found them a particularly valuable source of evidence. These instructional manuals provided the material for senior ethics courses that were intended, as John Dewey once observed, as "a kind of intellectual coping to the structure erected in earlier years, or, at least, as the insertion of the key-stone of the arch."[1] The course was designed to bring all knowledge into a proper moral focus, instilling in the nation's educated class an enlightened respect for basic Christian beliefs and virtues and shaping the character of her future leaders. It was virtually impossible for a person born in the first sixty years of the nineteenth century and educated in the American colleges to escape the influence of the course in moral philosophy. To become familiar with the central core of that ethical instruction is to learn something of the principles that Americans thought it important to teach themselves. These texts, therefore, present us with the official ethic of nineteenth-century America, and acquaint us with a system of values that is not without influence even in our own day.

A word of caution is necessary at the start. The term

"values" is an ambiguous one. One may, for instance, identify a person's values with what he in fact desires or seems to desire on the basis of his actions. Thus Alexis de Tocqueville, observing the American people in the early nineteenth century, was struck with their restless pursuit of wealth and their "taste for physical gratifications." Or one may identify a person's values with what he thinks he ought to desire, whether he actually desires it or not. A person busily engaged in making money may feel that his true ends in life should be of a higher order than the materialistic. In the case of a nation the matter is particularly complex. For a nation can propose for itself a body of ideals or goals that its citizens find it difficult to pursue resolutely or are reluctant to put into practice. Gunnar Myrdal, in his classic study of American egalitarian professions and racist attitudes, *The American Dilemma* (1944), documented one instance of this disparity between national ideals and practical realities. My study will concentrate on America's official ethic or public philosophy, and will treat those moral values that Americans thought they ought to desire.

To focus on a nation's official values, after having called attention to the contrast between these and what that nation desires in fact, invites irony. This is not my intention, although there are times when the disparity between profession and practice cannot be ignored. The Americans have not always lived up to their creed. Nations seldom do. But this is not to suggest that Americans do not take their official beliefs and values seriously. Indeed, one may, with equal plausibility, suggest that the Americans have sometimes taken their official ethic too seriously, that they have been overly idealistic and high-minded in their approach to social and political problems—a charge that has in fact frequently been made. In any event, my purpose here is mainly to examine the intellectual background of the American ethical creed, and to propose that in the colleges—in the study of moral philosophy—an especially noteworthy and determined effort was made to shape and instruct an American public conscience, to create an ethical frame of mind that would direct a new nation seeking a moral, as well as a political, identity in a changing world. Part of the irony involved in such an effort reflects the concerns of a nation seeking a higher law of morality in an age when all higher laws were coming into question. It is the irony of a people caught between ideals that they cannot relinquish and historical circumstances that they cannot deny. Such irony as this invites compassion as well as criticism: for we are superior to it only in retrospect.

In 1821 Ralph Waldo Emerson, an undergraduate at Harvard College, wrote a prize-winning essay, "The Present State of Ethical Philosophy." In this essay, Emerson announced that in the nineteenth century ethical studies would be called upon to perform an important social function. Noting the "disastrous effects" attending "the gradual demolition of the feudal system," of which the French Revolution was the most dramatically disastrous, he declared that modern society must depend on the wide dissemination of sound moral principles to ensure "the calm and secure possession of equal rights and laws." He was cheered by the fact that ethical studies had become more practical, less speculative than they had been in past ages. He was also given hope by what he described as "a leveling principle" in modern ethics, a celebration of the common virtues rather than spectacular and heroic feats. Finally, he applauded a rising popular interest in ethical questions, not just in the upper and middle classes, but even among "the lowest orders of the people." What is now needed, he advised, is some kind of formal consensus on the fundamental principles of morality, agreement on the meaning of basic moral terms, and the formation of a reasonably coherent code of moral maxims.[2] Emerson called for a public ethic to guide the liberated conscience.

Emerson's call was answered. In the American colleges in the mid-nineteenth century the question of fundamental moral principles was much labored, and a more or less consistent code of practical duties was in fact produced. The arena for this activity, the senior course in moral philosophy, was offered, together with a complementary course in "mental philosophy," as the highpoint of a young man's college education.[3] The results were often published in textbooks, based on lectures, which were usually entitled something like "Elements of Moral Philosophy [or "Moral Science"], Theoretical and Practical." The writers of these texts, mostly college presidents, many of them clergymen, sought to instruct their students—and their nation—in what was described as "the Science of What Ought to Be." They thought of themselves as providing needed moral leadership for their country.

We are especially concerned with a central group of these writers whom, for convenience, we shall call the academic moralists. These are men like Francis Wayland of Brown University, Mark Hopkins of Williams College, and James McCosh of Princeton, who seem particularly to represent the tone and style of thinking and to express the assumptions that are most typical of academic moral philosophy in the old-time college.* Our attention will be focused not on the men themselves, however, but on their underlying concerns as these are revealed in their textbooks and lectures on moral philosophy. The period with which we shall be dealing began in the 1830's, with the publication of Francis Wayland's *Elements of Moral Science* (1835). Wayland's book exhibits the form that subsequent moral philosophy textbooks were to follow, a matter that will concern us later. The era fades shortly after the Civil War, when most of the men in whom we are interested—and who were born around 1800—were either dead or past their prime. Nevertheless, the texts continued to come from the presses, either as revisions of earlier editions or as belated publications of lectures delivered years before. As late as 1892 McCosh published *Our Moral Nature Being a Brief System of Ethics*. This short and unoriginal work may be regarded as the last example of the genre.

"Moral Philosophy" was defined in the *Encyclopaedia Americana* in 1849 as "the science which treats the motives and rules of human actions, and of the ends to which they

---

* For biographical sketches of the major figures considered, see Appendix I.

ought to be directed." Although distinct from theology, it teaches of a "moral law" enacted by the "Supreme Legislator," and therefore points beyond itself in the direction of the Creator of the universe.[4] This definition is representative, and contains several noteworthy elements. To begin with, moral philosophy was not considered merely an analytical discipline, like modern ethics, but a study of the "ends" toward which our actions "ought to be directed." Its aim was not to arrive at some interpretative conclusions, but to come to a moral judgment, a statement of duty. As it was taught in the American colleges, moral philosophy was in fact frankly exhortative, intended more to instruct the conscience than to stimulate the intellect.

Second, moral philosophy was considered at once distinct from theology and related to religion. This raised special problems. An early academic moralist, John Witherspoon, the president of Princeton in the early years of the republic, had to defend the discipline against those who spoke of moral philosophy as "just reducing infidelity to a system" by appealing to reason rather than Scripture. "If Scripture is true, the discoveries of reason cannot be contrary to it," he maintained; "and therefore it has nothing to fear from that quarter."[5] There was something innovative, even daring, about teaching moral philosophy independently of theology. Once this independence had been established, of course, the results of the study could be offered as evidence in support of certain basic religious truths, such as the existence and moral attributes of God.

Third, moral philosophy is described as a "science." The men who taught the course maintained that they were not engaged in mere speculation, that they were indeed approximating the rigor of the physical sciences in their study of "the motives and rules of human actions." To their minds, effective teaching and exhortation demanded that their moral theories have the appearance of certainty; and the criterion of certainty was that of science. The enemy was speculative doubt concerning the fundamental principles of religion and morality. So it was considered appropriate that science, education, and exhortation join forces to arrest the advance of an enemy that threatened not only faith but moral conduct and philosophical good sense as well. To put the matter somewhat differently, the writers of the moral-philosophy textbooks wanted what Charles Sanders Peirce calls *belief*. But they realized that a belief, to be tenable in their age, could no longer be founded on unquestioned authority, but had to be founded on reason and science—had, in fact, to be a "true" belief, a belief that puts doubt to rest.[6] The science of morals, insofar as it could provide a sense of certainty in areas of ultimate concern, could offer sanity and peace, and could thus mitigate the "disastrous effects" attending the collapse of traditional regulatory institutions.

The old textbooks on moral philosophy may be found today in almost any college library, dusty and deteriorating, and somehow looking piteously out of place among recent ethical monographs. Some words of explanation are called for in approaching these superannuated texts. Their authors were men with a wide range of concerns and professional duties, and were frequently much better than the textbooks they wrote. As William James once observed, "an American college president is a very peculiar type of character, partly man of business, partly diplomatist, partly clergyman, and partly professor of metaphysics. . . ."[7] In most cases, such men did not have much time to work over their philosophical theories. And their treatises were occasioned more by pedagogical demands than by philosophical interest. Still, the textbooks appeared in impressive number, and they reflected deeper concerns than those of the hack textbook writer interested only in literary royalties or academic advancement. Moral philosophy in the mid-nineteenth century included not only ethics but most of the social sciences as well; it was closely related to the subject-matter of mental philosophy, which included psychology, epistemology, and arm-chair anthropology. The college course in moral philosophy, moreover, was designed to draw the higher learning together, providing students with what one historian has called a "unified interpretation of life."[8] The range of the course was thus axiological in the broadest sense, sweeping over a wide range of concerns, social and religious as well as ethical.

Upon examination, the textbooks turn out to be at once surprisingly narrow and surprisingly broad in their concerns. On the one hand, considering the fact that they were written by Protestant clergymen at a time of increasing denominational self-consciousness, it is surprising to find in these texts so little noteworthy evidence of doctrinal allegiance—although it is obvious, for example, in the treatment of free will. Nor does one find evidence of especially wide reading in contemporary ethical and theological materials. On reflection, it is not really difficult to account for these omissions. The course in moral philosophy was not intended as a survey course in ethics. Consequently, except for dismissing a few "erroneous" theories, the writers did not feel called upon critically and systematically to account for other ethical systems than their own. The primary academic concern of the academic moralists was neither philosophical nor theological: they wanted to present a handy system of ethics that would comprehend most of the student's concerns and answer, as neatly as possible, a number of theoretical questions. Because the course was designed more to provide answers than to raise questions, it was generally felt that these answers should be phrased as broadly as possible, and not tied to any narrow sectarian theological or philosophical formulation.

From this broader view, on the other hand, the textbooks express many of the concerns of a nation and an age, and thus serve as useful cultural documents. Perhaps a major goal of the academic moralists, as teachers and exhorters as well as philosophers, was to accommodate the old to the new —to adapt the western tradition of Christian morals to the demands of a new and changing world. The need for such an accommodation seemed obvious. A cherished moral heritage was being threatened by modern thought and society; and the expansive American republic needed whatever moral guidance such a heritage might provide. The meaning of the textbooks is thus best sought not in their logic but in their tone and in the assumptions and attitudes they express. On the broadest view, they represent modern man's effort to accept innovation without abandoning tradition; and in this respect they reveal a point of view that is forward-looking as well as conservative. More narrowly, they were intended to meet the need of which young Emerson spoke in 1821: to clarify and codify basic moral principles, and, in shaping the character and beliefs of the country's educated class, to help direct its moral progress. These textbooks in moral philosophy set forth a coherent system of ideas with which to instruct the public conscience of Victorian America. And if the texts themselves are now forgotten, the influence of their moral perspective extends beyond the century in which they were written.

Part One

The Teaching
of Moral Philosophy

1

Moral Philosophy
and Its Uses

"In North America the last traces of medieval feudalism disappear," Philip Schaff observed in 1855, excepting only Southern slavery. There is, he said, no king, nobility, or privileged class, no entailed estates, established church, or standing army. And yet, despite the openness of American society and the freedom it allows, there is "a universal respect for right and law; deep reverence for Christianity; a conservative spirit; well-ordered government; perfect security of person and property; and great independence, too, towards other nations."[1] Schaff's remark is instructive. What America lacked in traditional external institutions she compensated for in internal qualities of mind. It is noteworthy that, with the exception of a well-ordered government, all the items on the positive side of Schaff's ledger—"respect," "reverence," "independence," "a conservative spirit"—are traits of character and what were commonly labeled moral characteristics. In America, it was often observed, where the coercive regulatory institutions of medieval Europe never took root, freedom rested "upon a moral groundwork," and morality became, in Francis Grund's words, "the common law of the country."[2]

Formal education was one agent that helped create this salubrious state of affairs. Horace Mann, one of the best-known educators in the early republic, often insisted that education in this country must serve a moral as well as a practical and purely intellectual purpose. If our institutions "wake up the unexampled energies in the whole mass of the people," he once warned, then they must also "confer upon that people unexampled wisdom and rectitude," and direct the "higher faculties" while liberating the lower ones.[3] Moral education, to be sure, began in the home, with the Christian nurture the child presumably received there, but it extended through his years in Sunday School and in the public or preparatory schools. For those who went to college, those who would one day become society's most influential citizens, moral education continued on what was considered a more sophisticated level. The American system of higher education in the nineteenth century has been aptly described as "Protestant Scholasticism" because of its ambitious effort "to organize all knowledge, including knowledge of the cosmos, of man, and of society, into a consistent and intelligible whole," establishing a correspondence between secular knowledge and basic Christian principles.[4] The senior-year course in moral philosophy, joining education, inspiration, and exhortation, was designed to cap this system. It was intended to produce not the analytical mind but the committed intellect, the pious heart, and the dedicated will.

The mission of moral philosophy in the old-time college is perhaps best described by Noah Porter of Yale in an early essay, "Moral Science, as a Branch of Academical Education."[5] Writing in 1834, Porter lamented the fact that moral philosophy was not given sufficient attention in the colleges, and that the moral philosopher was looked down upon by students of political economy as "the least productive of the unproductive class." In countering this attitude, Porter compared moral "science" with natural science, noting that moral science describes man's relation to the moral order of the universe, just as astronomy describes earth's relation to the solar system. (This was to become a favorite textbook analogy.) Thus moral science is as important to the functioning of society as astronomy is to the guidance of a ship at sea; and the moral philosopher is a kind of moral "navigator" for

4

his country. "In a word," said Porter, "moral science gives every advantage to the christian, which natural science imparts, when she blesses man with the arts."[6] Moral science provides the theoretical background necessary for social engineering. It does this primarily by investigating and analyzing "the moral constitution of man" through the process of "reflection"—the thoroughgoing introspective examination of the mind. From the study of the mind, moral science opens out to include almost every area of human existence, dealing not only with theory but with "the warm and active realities of daily life." An especially important function of moral science is that of bringing the Christian message to educated men, who presumably can be reached no other way. "Would we preach the gospel to them with effect," Porter advised, "we must do it through their instructors in this department of knowledge." Once the educated class has been converted, then, through it, moral science must pass into "every portion of the community," to serve as an offensive weapon against scepticism and as a backstay to the social order.

Especially noteworthy is Porter's haste to draw the analogy between moral and natural science, his conviction that moral philosophy serves a religious function in helping convert intellectuals, and his élitism in regarding the moral philosopher as society's moral navigator and in looking to educated men as the custodians of their nation's values. Jefferson to the contrary notwithstanding, the ploughman must ultimately come to the professor for moral guidance. The course in moral philosophy, assimilating modern ideas and working through the nation's educated class, was expected to civilize and redeem American society.

On perhaps a more mundane level moral philosophy was intended to help the old-time college perform its most important function, the essentially conservative task of providing "intellectual stability and order in a fluid society."[7] The college, in performing this service, was often criticized for not adjusting its curriculum to the practical demands of the times—a charge that cannot be casually dismissed, although one might well marvel that an institution, so much a part of

5

bustling community life, so limited in its resources, could represent as well as it did its intellectual heritage. Indeed, it could be argued that nineteenth-century America needed models of cultural integrity at least as much as she needed more examples of creative adaptability; and that perhaps the old-time college and its faculty best served American society by resisting most of its demands.[8] In any case, the task of providing intellectual stability and order involved a measure of philosophical reconstruction. For, as Walter Houghton observes in his detailed examination of the Victorian frame of mind, "while moral values were firm until 1870, all intellectual theories, including those of morality, were insecure."[9] In the United States, it fell to the professor of moral philosophy to make secure the intellectual theory behind moral values. Conscientiously, if not always judiciously or comprehensively, he read ethical treatises, and set forth a consistent system of ethics that met his pedagogical needs and justified what he considered the fundamental moral values. Needless to say, the results, as they appeared in lectures and textbooks, were usually neither original nor profound. But, as Mark Hopkins ruefully observed, "to combine the qualities of a good text-book with original investigation is not easy."[10] The course in moral philosophy represents a diligent attempt to accommodate what was precious from the past to the needs, intellectual as well as social, of a new and changing world.

In spite of Noah Porter's complaint in 1834 that moral philosophy was the object of academic contempt, the course had a venerable tradition. It was prominent in the medieval curriculum, it was taught in the English and Scottish universities, and it had been adopted at both Harvard and William and Mary in seventeenth-century America. In the eighteenth century, George P. Schmidt remarks, moral philosophy "through sheer inertia became as common a feature of the average American college as the president's house and the treasury deficit."[11]

Of the American textbooks on moral philosophy published in the eighteenth and early nineteenth centuries, that by

Thomas Clap of Yale is fairly representative,[12] but for the most part the Americans tended to look to Britain for their texts. Following the Revolution, one of the most widely available and useful British books on moral philosophy was Archdeacon William Paley's *Moral and Political Philosophy* (1785). This work became the standard textbook in most American colleges in the post-revolutionary period.[13] Paley's ethical theory offered nothing original. But it did present a unique rephrasing of many old ideas; and, joined in one prodigious volume with his *Evidences of Christianity* (1794) and his *Natural Theology* (1802), it remained on American college library shelves long after its influence had waned in the 1830's. The popularity of Paley's theological writings is understandable. His *Evidences* offered a readable, non-sectarian defense of New-Testament revelation. And his *Natural Theology*, with its famous time-piece analogy to prove the divine contrivance of the universe, compensated for its unoriginality by its tidy summation of the prevailing arguments for the existence and glorious attributes of God. We can only conjecture what influence his moral theory, which was utilitarian, actually had in the United States.[14]

It seems most likely that American academicians in the post-revolutionary period simply found Paley's *Moral and Political Philosophy* convenient, and adopted it as a textbook without ever being committed to its utilitarian theory. To be sure, later critics were inclined to cite the wide use of Paley's text as an example of the lamentable state of moral philosophy in the United States before 1835.[15] It must be remembered, however, that Paley's text offered a comprehensive discussion of the various points that the course was expected to cover; and it was readable and clear. Moreover, his utilitarianism was not narrowly hedonistic; and his entire theoretical system was lodged in the theologically secure moral government of God, with its just distribution of rewards and punishments. Finally, he made the will of God the ultimate basis of moral distinctions. In short, in elaborating his moral philosophy Paley drew on a well-established theological tradition, giving it the scientific lucidity of the utilitarian for-

7

mulation. America's inertia in producing its own textbooks and Paley's general availability and reliability account for the Archdeacon's popularity in this country.

Paley's ethical theory is easily summarized. He defined "virtue" as "doing good to mankind, in obedience to the will of God, and for the sake of everlasting happiness."[16] This definition, by assuming a coincidence between divine will and human interest, presumably satisfied the theologian and the man of refined principles while applying effective coercion to the person of baser motives. One is morally obligated, Paley argued, "when he is urged by a violent motive resulting from the command of another." He bluntly affirmed that his motive must be "violent," for we "can be obliged to nothing, but what we ourselves are to gain or lose something by."[17] If we agree with this, what difference is there between mere prudence and moral duty? "The difference, and the only difference" between prudence and duty, Paley insisted, is that "in the one case, we consider what we shall gain or lose in the present world; in the other, we consider also what we shall gain or lose in the world to come." Duty, then, was nothing more than prudence in a cosmic perspective. Paley concluded that his reasoning proves that there can be no obligation, and hence no true "system of morality," without a religious belief in the life after death.[18]

Such was the substance of Paley's theory. The reasoning was simple; the appeal to self-interest could reach all but the most dissolute sensibilities; and the entire argument seemed to confirm some of the fundamental beliefs of religion. Nevertheless, evangelical Protestants could find little comfort in Paley's outspoken utilitarianism, with its unblushing appeal to selfish motives.[19] More fundamentally, Paley's ethical theory was open to serious philosophical criticism. It offered an inadequate account of moral obligation: why, for example, is man morally obligated to seek his own everlasting happiness? By making God's will the basis of right, it provided a questionable criterion for moral distinctions: can any arbitrary will, even God's, be the basis of right? Finally, in the opinion of many, it presented an unsatisfactory description of virtue: Paley's virtue was only selfishness bridled by fear. After 1835 American academicians abandoned Paley's moral theory, no longer content merely to qualify it from the lecture platform as they had previously done. Nor did they merely dispense with Paley, without ever bothering to refute him. In the American texts on moral philosophy all the failings of the Paleyan system were pointed out, including its unsatisfactory treatment of obligation, moral distinctions, and virtue.[20]

To be sure, there was no ceremony involved in abandoning Paley. None was required. An outdated textbook had simply been replaced on the reading list. In a somewhat haphazard way American academicians supplemented Paley (or whatever text they were using) until they had supplanted him, and thus inaugurated the "textbook era" in American ethics.[21] The example of Francis Wayland, whose *Elements of Moral Science* appeared in 1835, shows how supplementary views grew into independent theory:

> These views, for my own convenience, I soon committed to paper, and delivered in the form of lectures. In a few years these lectures had become so far extended that, to my surprise, they contained by themselves the elements of a different system from that of the textbook which I was teaching.[22]

Despite these casual beginnings, Wayland's text was the subject of a certain nationalistic pride. Its appearance was hailed in both Cambridge and Princeton as the opening of a new era, and it seemed an answer to Noah Porter's complaint a year before that the moral philosopher in America was looked down upon as the least productive of the unproductive class.[23]

Wayland's textbook displayed the general form that American texts in moral philosophy were to follow after 1835. It was divided between "Theoretical Ethics" and "Practical Ethics," the latter detailing man's various moral and political duties and constituting about two thirds of the book. Wayland's "Theoretical Ethics" dealt with the nature of morality and with man's "moral constitution." His concern with the epistemology of morals and with the problem of defining the "moral quality" of actions distinguishes him

9

from most of his American predecessors. Others had treated these matters, to be sure.[24] But Wayland, and those who followed him, exhibited a new concern about the rationality of our moral judgments and a new awareness of the uniqueness of such moral problems as how we come to recognize a specifically moral obligation. Wayland's text is distinguished, further, by its didactic and social concern. "Being designed for the purpose of instruction," Wayland declared in his Preface,

> its aim is to be simple, clear, and purely didactic. I have rarely gone into extended discussion, but have contented myself with the attempt to state the moral law, and the reasons for it, in as few and as comprehensive terms as possible.[25]

Perhaps here we have a clue to the real significance of the academic moralists. Beginning in the eighteenth century, as Norman Fiering has observed, moral philosophy served as a "semi-secular way station" between a world dominated by theology and one dominated by science.[26] It provided a common intellectual basis for discussing what William James once called the deepest reasons of the universe. In the appearance of the academic moralists we witness a formalization of this discussion, an effort to define the terms used and even to forespeak the conclusions to be reached. Such formalization seemed essential to the health and stability of the republic. To put it another way, if the rise of moral philosophy in the eighteenth century is to be considered a manifestation of the Enlightenment, then the appearance of textbook moralism in the nineteenth century may be considered an attempt to make the Enlightenment safe for democracy. Textbook moralism was an effort to appropriate the energies of the modern mind for the public welfare. As an academic pursuit, said Francis Bowen in his review of Wayland's text, moral philosophy "may be highly valuable in the veriest utilitarian sense." For it is concerned with the responsible instruction of the conscience in an age and country where such instruction is essential, but neglected.[27]

Like Noah Porter, Wayland and those who followed him were aware of their social significance as academic moral

10

philosophers. They were, if not their society's moral navigators, important figures in a free and open society—a society,
it was often observed, that depended for its order and sur-
vival not on force but on the "virtue and intelligence" of its
citizens. It was the task of the academic moralists to see to it
that the traditional rules of virtue were not forgotten. This
they were to do by defending the old virtues in terms comprehensible to nineteenth-century Americans and then persuading their countrymen to live the virtuous life, making
morality the "common law of the country." They would thus
serve both their nation and the cause of righteousness.
Clearly, academic moral philosophers need not remain the
least productive of the unproductive class.

2

Representative Men

The limits of generalization become immediately clear from a simple survey of the broader social and intellectual purposes of the college textbooks on moral philosophy. The writers of these texts were unquestionably a diverse group both philosophically and theologically, and they can be considered collectively only in their office as college teachers concerned to instruct the public conscience through what was often called "character education." Even with this limited focus in mind, it is useful to take note of some of the differences among the individuals that compose the group, particularly with respect to basic ethical and theological assumptions; and the most satisfactory way of doing this is to examine the central ideas of a few representative men, such as Francis Wayland, Mark Hopkins, Francis Bowen, and Archibald Alexander.

Francis Wayland (1796–1865)[1] was born in New York City, the son of a leather merchant. After graduation from Union College in 1813, he studied medicine for a time, but finally decided to enter the Baptist ministry. After a year of study at Andover and a brief career in the parish ministry in Boston, he went to Brown University, where he served as president from 1827 until 1855, gaining a reputation as an educational reformer through his efforts to improve the Brown curriculum.[2] His *Elements of Moral Science*, published in 1835, was an extremely popular work, running through many printings and selling more than 100,000

13

copies.[3] Far less popular were his texts *Political Economy* (1837) and *Intellectual Philosophy* (1854), which dealt respectively with economics and psychology as subjects complementary to moral science.

Wayland was evangelical in religion and a moderate Calvinist in theology. He expressed his theological position in a letter of 1861:

> I am a moderate Calvinist. The sharp angles of Calvinism, which need to be filed and hammered out in order to make a system, I desire to hold no opinion about. It seems to me that the fault of all theological systems arises from logical consequences drawn from some revealed truth. Now, for this sort of logic, I have no sort of respect.

The truths of revelation are divine and "not proper subjects for human logic." He demonstrated this, significantly, by showing the "absurdity" of attempting logically to relate divine sovereignty to man's free agency.[4] The matter of free agency was of particular concern for Wayland as a moralist and preacher. He had insisted, earlier, that the Scriptural doctrine of total depravity does not mean that man is totally evil with no element of good. "The principles of ethics would teach us that such a view is erroneous."[5] The inability of logic to cope with the mystery of revelation has been a theme of theologians since Augustine, of course; and so there seems, at first glance, nothing new in what Wayland was saying. What is significant is that, even though the Word of God might drive logic to "absurdity," it would never contradict the "principles of ethics." Moral responsibility implies free agency, or, in the handy modern formula, "ought" implies "can." The fact is that the truths of revelation were being translated into the common-sense language of a new ethical outlook in which nice theological distinctions might be blurred and paradoxes could not be tolerated.

Wayland's moral theory, with certain pious qualifications, was what is today called intuitionist and "deontological" as opposed to "teleological."* For him, such moral distinctions

---

* For a fuller discussion of the meaning of these ethical terms, see Appendix II.

as right and wrong arise in uniquely moral "relations," are apprehended intuitively, and are not translatable into other, non-moral, terms. Right is right in itself, independent of any other consideration.[6] One is morally obligated to do what is right, not because it conduces to some good or is divinely enjoined, but because it is perceived to be right under the circumstances. The marriage relationship, for example, places responsibilities on both the man and the wife. A wife is obliged to submit to her husband not because God so commands her (although Wayland threw this in too), but because submission is the fitting attitude for a woman in the marriage relation. Wayland tried to place God above all this, thereby drawing the fire of Francis Bowen.[7] By his definition, the relation of man to God includes all other relations,[8] but it is clear that the duty of a wife to her husband would have existed even if there had been no God.

The ethical theories on which Wayland relied, earlier elaborated by British moralists such as Joseph Butler and Dugald Stewart, contradicted many of the fundamental principles of strict Calvinist theology. It is little wonder that Wayland was forced to file off and hammer out the "sharp angles" of Calvinist orthodoxy. But, as he himself once said, it was not a consistent theology so much as a "Consistent Piety" that was "the Demand of the Age."[9] Wayland's purpose was not to maintain sharp theological distinctions but to teach morals and to "urge upon individual Christians . . . a more consistent and uncompromising profession of religion."[10] Purity of heart counts more than purity of doctrine.

The possibly explosive combination of an ethical obligation to do right regardless of consequences and an evangelical call for "consistent and uncompromising" piety was modified by Wayland's own conservative temperament. Wayland contemplated neither kicking over the social order nor abandoning tradition. In his book *Limitations of Human Responsibility*, published three years after *Moral Science*, Wayland argued that, although the authority of the conscience is "unquestionable," and "no earthly motive" ought to "interfere with the discharge of my duty," nevertheless one may—and must—ask, "Has conscience really com-

15

manded?" and "What is, and what is not, my duty?"[11] Wayland's cautious stand on social issues, including slavery, is sufficient testimony to his basic conservatism. As he was willing to bend theology to meet the demands of ethics, so he was willing to bend ethics to match his conservatism. The moral order must remain, above all, orderly.

Mark Hopkins (1802–87),[12] the grandnephew of the theologian Samuel Hopkins, was born in Stockbridge, Massachusetts. He attended Williams College, studied medicine, and struggled along as a doctor in New York for nearly three years. Unhappy in the medical profession, he accepted an appointment in 1831 as Professor of Moral Philosophy and Rhetoric at Williams College. Although he had never attended a theological school, he was ordained a Congregational minister in 1836, and that same year was elected president of Williams, where he remained until his death. He did not publish his *Lectures on Moral Science* until 1862. These were followed, in 1869, by *The Law of Love and Love as a Law*, which presented essentially the same moral theory, but with some clarification and greater attention to practical ethics.

Hopkins's religion, despite denominational differences, was not significantly different from Wayland's. He modified the consistent Calvinism of his great-uncle, and set out in the "great work of interpreting Christianity in such a way as to retain all its great emotional appeal and free it from the dark shadow of the old Calvinist dogma."[13] He never explicitly abandoned the old creed, however. It was simply that the old terrors lost their urgency for him.

Mark Hopkins was not a scholar. In 1870 he admitted that he had "not the faintest glimmer" of what many of the writers on metaphysics were talking about.[14] In a letter to Noah Porter in the mid-1880's, he disarmingly confessed:

> When I was elected as Professor [in 1830–31], I bought a poor translation of Kant, but soon gave it up in despair, and have not attempted him since.[15]

His despair of understanding Kant, however, did not prevent him from citing that philosopher in lectures whenever he wished to exhibit "specimens of nonsense" in his classes.[16] However meager a reading it was based upon, Hopkins's moral theory is worthy of consideration, for his ethical textbooks were widely used in colleges in the later nineteenth century.[17] His position was teleological but not narrowly utilitarian. He referred moral distinctions and obligation to a non-moral end, the "supreme good," which all men ought to seek, and which is based on man's nature and mental constitution. Hopkins said:

> If the human constitution was made by a wise and good being, it must have been made for certain ends; and in these ends, whatever they may be, and nowhere else, can its perfection and happiness be found. To discover these ends and the means of attaining them, is the object of moral philosophy.[18]

Each faculty of mind has its own legitimate end; and all, working together in harmony, have as their collective end the promotion of the "supreme good"—the happiness of God and of the sentient universe.[19]

Like Wayland, Hopkins wanted ethical certainty in a changing world. He argued his case not by referring to external moral relations, as did Wayland, but by concentrating on human nature conceived as a purposeful whole. By taking this view of human nature, Hopkins arrived at a moral theory that appears almost as uncompromising as Wayland's. Man must be fully himself, said Hopkins. But man's true self is a zealously committed self, each faculty containing a built-in imperative. While Wayland perceived unyielding imperatives in certain relations, Hopkins discovered no less demanding imperatives in the human constitution. Neither offered much room for moral compromise. And it was only because Hopkins was as conservative in temperament as Wayland that he could keep his implicit perfectionism in check. Confronted with such explosive issues as slavery and women's rights, Hopkins was forced to short-circuit his logical order in the interest of social order.[20] Thus the theoretical differences between Wayland and Hopkins are not fundamental; in practice they are one.

Francis Bowen (1811–90) differed from Wayland and

17

Hopkins in several respects. He was a Unitarian. He was not a clergyman. He did not publish a textbook on moral philosophy, although he did produce one on the related subject of political economy in 1856; his published Lowell *Lectures* of 1848–49 adequately set forth his views on both ethics and natural theology.[21] Unitarian though he was, Bowen was an intellectual conservative. His main concern as a philosopher was to provide respectable intellectual support for traditional moral principles, and to offer a philosophical defence of basic Christian truths.[22] In this respect he resembles Wayland, Hopkins, and the other academic moralists.

Born in Charlestown, Massachusetts, to parents with limited financial resources, Bowen had difficulty putting himself through preparatory school and college. Graduated from Harvard in 1833, he was able to study for a year in Europe. In 1843 he succeeded John Gorham Palfrey as editor of the *North American Review*, and soon gained a reputation both as an outspoken political conservative and as an astute critic of the thought of such philosophers as Locke, Kant, Fichte, and Victor Cousin.[23] In 1853 he was appointed Alford Professor of Natural Religion, Moral Philosophy, and Political Economy at Harvard, replacing James Walker in that distinguished post. Although remembered mainly for his writings on political economy, Bowen has justly been described as "the most competent philosopher at Harvard before the coming of George Herbert Palmer, Josiah Royce, and William James."[24]

As a Unitarian, Bowen differed in many ways from the theological doctrine of Wayland and Hopkins. Nevertheless, beneath the doctrinal disagreement and the persistent animosity still evident in New England in the 1840's, there was a broad base of agreement between the more conservative Unitarians, like Bowen, and their orthodox brethren. In theology, Calvinists and Unitarians had clashed most vigorously over the ethical question of man's responsibility with respect to grace,[25] the very question that was now fragmenting orthodoxy itself. Moreover, Unitarianism, still largely confined to the greater Boston area, was anxious to prove its own orthodoxy by renouncing all the latest forms of infidelity, such as Transcendentalism.[26] Conservative Unitarians shared with moderate orthodoxy the same social ethic, the same underlying moral concerns. And there were even signs, in the 1840's, of a growing rapprochement between evangelicals and conservative Unitarians.[27]

In ethical theory, Unitarian thinkers, less hampered by confessional commitments than Calvinists, could afford to insist more emphatically than their orthodox counterparts on the independence of ethics from doctrinal theology. Bowen could expose the jagged sectarian edges of Wayland's moral theory to demonstrate "the necessity of keeping the department of Ethics distinct from that of Dogmatic Theology."[28] Bowen himself, however, did not contemplate a secularized ethics completely independent of religion. His Lowell lectures reveal his major concern. The *Lectures* deal with "natural theology," which treats the existence and attributes of God, and "natural religion," which discloses God's moral purpose and acquaints man with his duty.[29] Both these disciplines, said Bowen, are empirical "sciences," treating matters of fact rather than *a-priori* relations between ideas. Bowen wanted to make morals scientifically certain, and to prove that the natural world is morally purposeful. To do the latter, he argued that the "laws" of nature imply not mechanical necessity but the continuing agency of God, the moral governor, in nature. To do the former, he made conscience the ethical counterpart of Providence or divine agency, giving it the unique power unerringly (provided it remain "unperverted") to distinguish right from wrong, and emphasizing its absolute authority over human conduct.

Bowen resembles Mark Hopkins in his effort to demonstrate, through a scientific examination of the human mind, the moral government of the universe. But he ended up with a deontological moral theory that was more dependent on the immediate testimony of the conscience than was Wayland's. Conscience, said Bowen, is a separate faculty of mind, the "inlet" of simple ideas of right and wrong that are *sui generis*. Moral distinctions, he insisted, are absolutely

19

independent of God's will: "We do not do right because God commands it, but God commands it because it is right."[30] The shoe pinched at two points. In the first place, if moral distinctions are independent of God's will, God is not truly sovereign. Like most academic moral philosophers, particularly Unitarian moralists,[31] Bowen was willing to qualify God's omnipotence in order to preserve an independent standard of right and wrong. This maneuver forestalled the possibility that the moral law might be, in any sense, arbitrary; and it placed Bowen in a position to assert the goodness of God. But it also prompted at least one critic to maintain that Bowen's god was not really God at all, and that Bowen was little more than an atheist.[32] In the second place, depending as he did on the testimony of (unperverted) conscience, Bowen could not explain precisely what relation obtains between our subjective apprehension of the moral law and its objective content. Is an action right because conscience says it is, or is it right in itself irrespective of conscience? Desiring to ground moral distinctions both on certain knowledge and on absolute law, Bowen ended with a notion of moral duty that was as unyielding as Wayland's or Hopkins, even though Bowen was at least as conservative as they.

Bowen was somewhat atypical of academic moralists in his theological liberalism. Archibald Alexander (1772–1851),[33] a Virginia-born Old School Presbyterian, was atypical in his theological conservatism. Alexander was the first professor at the Princeton Theological Seminary when it opened in 1812. He was a friend and colleague of the contentious Charles Hodge, lifelong defender of the Westminster Confession. The Princeton men were ardent opponents of what they deemed the Arminian tendencies—the progressive displacement of divine grace by human will—of the New England theology as represented by most Congregationalists and by the New School Presbyterians.

Alexander's textbook on moral philosophy was based on seminary lectures designed "as a transition from college work and a recapitulation of juvenile studies."[34] His moral theory seems almost a combination of the ideas of Mark

Hopkins, Wayland, and Bowen. He began with the conscience, which, he said, distinguishes right from wrong, establishes the fact of obligation, and evokes appropriate feelings of approbation and blame. He insisted that virtue and
vice are *sui generis* and indefinable; and he specifically at-
tacked the Edwardsean definition of "virtue" as "disinterested benevolence." Alexander was anxious to show that all
men, even atheists, have a conscience: for conscience is the
evidence of God's existence and the proof, within each human breast, of God's moral perfection.[35] Like Mark Hopkins, Alexander started with the moral powers of man. Like
Wayland and Bowen, he elaborated a deontological moral
theory. And he was even more of an intuitionist than Bowen
in trusting the direct testimony of conscience and in refusing
to define the uniquely moral ideas it presents. Like Bowen,
also, Alexander used moral philosophy as a tool of natural
theology, to prove the existence and goodness of God. More
clearly than any of these men, Alexander exhibited his doctrinal concerns in his philosophy.

Alexander's Calvinism is evident mainly in his treatment
of the will. In order to preserve divine sovereignty in the
face of human responsibility, Alexander endorsed the approach of Jonathan Edwards, tracing volitions back to
"affections," "desires," and an underlying "disposition" to
behave in one way or another. He employed the old formula
that a person is free to do what he will, but not to will what
he will.[36] In doing this, he kept human volitions from becoming an independent variable in God's dependent universe.
This was good Calvinism, to be sure. But it extended human
responsibility far beyond the range of voluntary action, and
came close to violating the ethical maxim that "ought" implies "can." Bowen's philosophy embarrassed his theology,
while Alexander's theology confused his philosophy.

The differences among Wayland, Hopkins, Bowen, and
Alexander are at once evident. In religious doctrine, we find
Bowen and Alexander on the edges, representing Unitarian-
ism and strict Calvinism respectively, and Wayland and
Hopkins the more common moderate Calvinist position.
Among moderate Calvinists, the fundamental theological

variations concerned the meaning of free will and the definition of virtue. With respect to virtue, some, like Mark Hopkins, followed in the Edwardsean tradition and spoke of
virtue as a solemn, life-long commitment to the principle of
universal benevolence; while others, like Wayland, preferred a wider definition of virtue—one that includes, besides
benevolence, an explicit commitment to justice or reciprocity.[37] There were variations in ethical theory, running from
the strict deontological theory of Alexander to the teleological theory of Hopkins, while Wayland actually combined
elements of both.[38] There was disagreement about the mix-
ing of religion and ethics, mainly concerning the intrusion
of doctrinal theology into ethical theory. Nevertheless, most
academic moralists, including Wayland and Alexander,
agreed that Christian faith and ethics, though ultimately
related—the latter proving the former—were distinct.

The similarities among these men are more striking,
however, than their differences. All were committed to Protestant Christianity; none wanted a totally neutral ethical
theory like that of Richard Hildreth or Immanuel Kant. All
spoke with reference to the Calvinist theology, even those
like Bowen who opposed it. All found it difficult to reconcile
religious conviction and ethical theory. All repudiated utilitarianism in both its secular and crasser theological formulations, represented by Bentham and Paley respectively. All,
with significant variations, related ethics to some theory of
the human mind. All developed ethical theories that made
moral compromise difficult, while at the same time tending
to make all issues questions of morality. Finally, and most
important, all sought to offer a philosophical restatement of
fundamental moral truths—truths that they regarded as
eternal and unchanging. Men could move confidently into
the modern world if they remained in touch with the world
that was everlasting. The American academic moralists represent nineteenth-century man's philosophical quest for certainty.

3

Assumptions and Attitudes

Surveying the philosophy and letters of the mid-nine-teenth century, one observes men striving, like Tantalus, toward a goal that their very effort seems to put beyond reach. The Mid-Victorians believed that they could translate an old morality into a new language without fundamentally altering its meaning, that a new intellectual system could preserve traditional moral values. Their job was frustrating if not self-defeating. It is thus understandable that the writing of the American academic moralists reveals many inconsistencies. Yet it would be unfair to present their thought, as displayed in the ethical textbooks, with all its obvious contradictions, without first attempting to describe their *thinking*—the living concerns and worries behind the now cold record—taking note of the basic assumptions, allegiances, and mental attitudes that once made these contradictions seem reconcilable.[1] Such a description should include mention of the academic moralists' basically *a-priori* approach to the study of the mind, their religious commitment, their acceptance of science as the model of rational explanation, their belief in a transcendent moral law, and their peculiar combination of conservatism and radicalism.

I. *A-priori psychologism*. In spite of their celebration of the inductive method, the academic moralists dealt with human nature (by which they meant the human mind) in a deductive rather than an empirical or experimental way.

23

They abstracted "truths" about human nature from moral and religious assumptions that they regarded as axiomatic, made great display of "discovering" these truths as empirical "facts" in their own consciousness, and from these facts drew inferences about society, nature, and the moral universe. The fruits of this laborious process—the "fundamental truths" they deduced—were but the corollaries, and sometimes merely restatements, of those ethical and religious axioms with which they had begun their investigations. This circuitous exercise rested on certain methodological assumptions and a central teleological conviction that was regarded as being absolutely above question.

The methodological assumptions included the belief that the human mind, analyzed into its various "powers" or "faculties," was itself the most reliable guarantor of the first truths in epistemology and ethics. Disputed matters were referred to the "common sense" or "universal reason" of mankind as revealed in the convictions of all men, expressed in ordinary language, and represented in one's own consciousness. The validity of the technique of analogical reasoning, a recognized method of argument in natural theology that had been brought to its full development in the eighteenth century in Joseph Butler's famous *Analogy of Religion* (London, 1736), was also assumed. Its application in moral science was based on the belief that truth is one, and that the natural and moral universes, although distinct, are nonetheless in perfect harmony, so that a phenomenon in one area must have its counterpart in another. Natural and moral laws were considered to be fundamentally similar. The clockwork of the solar system, for example, is analogous to the moral order in human society, and inferences drawn from one system have at least qualified application in the other.

These assumptions—the authority of common sense, the reliability of consciousness, the validity of analogy—were supported by the conviction that the entire universe is presided over by a wise, benevolent, and all-powerful deity who has ingeniously contrived the whole operation to serve some moral purpose. This conviction met little really responsible opposition in the early nineteenth century; and many besides Emerson regarded the human mind as a kind of lens designed to concentrate the rays of God's moral law to a focus. The belief that man was psychologically adapted to fit into a morally purposive universe seemed, in fact, to have the universal assent of mankind.

II. *Religious moralism.* The academic moral philosophers were all deeply concerned with religion, that is, with Protestant Christianity. During the middle third of the nineteenth century, American Protestantism was going through a remarkable transition. The period opened in agitation and schism within the various churches, as the proponents of contending schools of theology struggled among themselves to establish the doctrinal identity of their denominations.[2] One of the most notable of these clashes took place in the Presbyterian and Congregational churches, between the so-called "old" and "new" divinity men, the former defending a traditional Calvinist orthodoxy and accusing the latter of the Arminian heresy of increasing man's self-determination at the expense of God's sovereignty. To be sure, the age was one of increasing denominational consolidation, but the denominations were far from being homogeneous units.[3] Further to complicate the situation, despite the denominational consciousness there was emerging in this period a generalized American Protestantism, characterized by a combination of moderate and evangelical Calvinism, and infused with elements of Enlightenment empiricism, romantic sentimentalism, and middle-class moralism. The emergence of this more liberal and accommodating Protestant spirit can be traced in the thinking of such prominent figures as Nathaniel William Taylor, Horace Bushnell, and Henry Ward Beecher.[4] Thus, while each denomination was struggling toward a sharper self-definition, Protestantism itself was being Americanized, and nineteenth-century America was becoming a Protestant civilization.

It was to this emerging Protestant conscience that the textbooks on moral philosophy made their deepest appeal. The texts drew a studiedly ambiguous line between divine sovereignty and human ability, stressed the need to cultivate

25

a devout heart as well as a good character, and spoke in behalf of a law of duty that was at once rationally apprehensible, compatible with Scriptural revelation, and expressive of the highest aspirations of the human soul. In a period in which theological systems were being refined to such an extent that the most subtle differences provoked major theological disputes, moral philosophy provided an intellectual common ground for an emerging liberal, evangelical Protestantism. In this respect, academic moral philosophy performed a good service for a nation in which sectarian division and doctrinal quarreling could not obscure the longing for an underlying moral and spiritual consensus.

Although most of the writers of the moral-philosophy textbooks and treatises considered ethics to be independent of dogmatic theology, they all assumed that faith and morals are related. As a Christian, the moral philosopher could appeal to the disinterested witness of man's moral nature in order to support the basic propositions of natural theology and to indicate the need for revealed truth. When theology and Scripture were put aside, and man was studied simply as a moral being, it was invariably discovered that the "voice of conscience is also the voice of God."[5] Religion returned this courtesy on the part of moral theory by supporting morality, since Christian belief supported good conduct. Faith in God, said Jasper Adams, and in "his superintending Providence, is alike the foundation of morals and religion," and the "deep sense of God" is "the root and branch of practical morals."[6] In morals, then, religion was eminently functional. Not only did it testify that the universe was, indeed, moral; but it also sanctioned private and public virtue, and provided, in God, "a fixed standard of moral excellence" as an inspiration for all right-thinking people.[7]

III. *Pious scientism.* The distinction between "science" and "philosophy" emerged only in the late eighteenth and early nineteenth centuries. The famous "warfare" between science and theology that so troubled the later nineteenth century is not to be sought, in the familiar form of two antagonistic authorities, in this period. The early Victorians, trying to heal the breach that had widened between faith

26

and reason for well over a century, were determined to demonstrate the unity of truth, and to show that science proved the truths of religion and morality. If theology was no longer the queen of the sciences, science would still remain the handmaid of religion. Truth is one: this Victorian axiom was the necessary precondition of the clash between theology and science after Darwin. For if truth is one, and religion is true, it follows that science must support religion, and religious belief must conform with scientific knowledge.

Science served both religion and morality by describing a purposeful cosmos and contributing to moral progress. It offered unimpeachable testimony that the universe ran according to a benevolent plan, that it was intelligently designed. Applied to the "arts," science promoted the material progress that was considered (albeit with some reservations) a vehicle of moral progress.[8] The American academic moralists shared the convictions and hopes of their generation. They were anxious to preserve traditional moral and religious values, to be sure; but they were also committed to the innovations, social and material, that were the fruit of applied science. And they were hopeful that the new truths of science would forever establish the everlasting Truth of faith.

IV. *Moral legalism.* Both the natural and the moral worlds were considered to be law-bound systems, legislated by God according to the law of His own being (not by an arbitrary act of will), and superintended by God to establish his glory and effect the ultimate redemption of mankind. For the academic moralists, the legal model of morality seems almost an obsession. And the frequent recurrence of the word "law" in the ethical textbooks makes the reader forget that the writers were American philosophers and think of them instead as Protestant Sadducees.

The term "moral law" was usefully ambiguous. "Law," as Henri Bergson observes, may denote either an imperative rule or an observed natural regularity;[9] and the American academicians were not always clear which they meant when they used the term. Furthermore, in the early nineteenth century "moral" had several meanings. The term could be

27

used to refer to what is ethically significant and worthy of praise or blame. But "moral" could also indicate an empirical rather than an *a-priori* method of reasoning, a "moral" science being an inductive science. Again, "moral" might refer simply to the human factor in any explanation of things —as when one speaks of the "moral" (human or volitional) influence in history, in contrast to the "natural" influence of catastrophes. To say, then, that a nation lives under a "moral law" could mean many things. It could mean that a nation lives under a divinely prescribed code, like the ancient Israelites. It could mean that a wicked nation, by the arrangement of things, cannot prosper. It could mean that the citizens of a nation have certain ethical obligations as well as purely legal duties. Or it could mean that a study of, for example, a nation's economy must consider certain volitional factors as well as general determining conditions: it must treat the nation's entrepreneurial spirit as well as its natural resources.

Interweaving and sometimes confusing the various meanings of "moral law," academic moralists could accomplish many things. They could shift their arguments from the indicative to the imperative, from "is" to "ought": morality could thus be approached as an inductive science, and the natural order could be expected to yield ethical values. Or they could move from the ethical to the metaphysical realm, referring questions of duty and obligation to some transcendent moral authority. Finally, because the moral law was both a "law of our being" and a "law of God," it conveniently tied methodology to ends: it was both a deduction from and a support of *a-priori* psychologism; and it connected the scientific study of the mind with Christian duty and Christian faith.

V. *Conservatism.* The word "conservatism" is difficult to define, especially when it is applied to the American experience. Among the many senses in which it is used, it may simply refer to the traditional Burkean position, with its reliance on long-standing traditions and institutions (including established religion) and its commitment to a hierarchical social order. Although this point of view has little political relevance in America, it is of some moral and literary significance. "Conservatism" may also refer to the nineteenth-century American blending of admiration for the business community and attachment to the principles of *laissez-faire*, at least as far as legislation to secure social justice is concerned. Or the term may be used to indicate an attitude of distrust of social change and fear for the future, frequently combined with a nostalgia for the contentments of some half-imagined past era. The matter is further complicated because Americans, it has frequently been observed, are at once radical and conservative—radical, for example, in their commitment to the social ideals set forth in the Preamble to the Declaration of Independence, yet temperamentally conservative in actively turning these ideals into social realities.[10]

To call the academic moralists conservatives is not to commit oneself to the claim that they were American Burkeans, or apologists for the business community, or backward-looking reactionaries—although many of them would fit one or more of these descriptions. For our purposes, "conservatism" refers to two things: a desire for order and stability in American republican institutions; and a commitment to traditional moral values. For the academic moralists, conservatism in the latter sense—that is, axiological conservatism—was entirely compatible with conservatism in the former sense. The preservation of traditional values, in fact, was regarded as a necessary condition for the maintenance of social stability. Moral philosophy, in a democratic society, was expected to perform, as we have already seen, much the same function as that performed by customs, traditions, and coercive institutions in more traditional European societies—to provide and implement moral values while restraining and directing men.

There was a basic flaw in these conservative premises. Since moral values and the transcendent moral law that sustains them command not only individuals but society as well, our moral philosophers were actually endorsing a principle that might be subversive of the social order they sought to guarantee. A higher law, unexpurgated of its right of revolution or its demand that men disobey immoral human laws, was cited in defense of social stability. And social morality became a matter to be settled between each well-meaning individual and God. Social and axiological conservatism may not be compatible after all: for the orderly society is seldom a righteous or just society.

VI. *Radicalism*. The moral philosophy textbooks were dry and dull. Their moral platitudes about good intentions were more than sufficiently bland, and their authors were, for the most part, temperamentally conservative. Yet in all this there was a radical element that must not escape notice. A moral theory based on the dictates of conscience offers little room for ethical compromise; and a commitment to a moral law that is above man's law would countenance the overthrow of iniquity at all costs. It takes more than logic to make men radical, however. Radicalism is more a product of the heart than of the head; and this was an age when the radical heart was encouraged. It is "the *Heart* which constitutes the *Man*," said the English evangelical, William Wilberforce, whose influential *Practical View* was reprinted in America every year during the first quarter of the nineteenth century. Our external actions "derive their whole character and meaning from the motives and dispositions of which they are indications." He urged all Christians earnestly to scrutinize their deepest feelings and desires.[11] This evangelical emphasis on the committed heart, combined with the insistence on the faithful performance of moral duty, with the long-standing Puritan emphasis on the need for continuous and anxious soul-searching, and with the popular literary fascination with sentiment, led many to the conclusion that disinterested moral vehemence and sacrificial devotion to a good cause were essential to good character.

The senior classes were instructed in mental and moral philosophy and indoctrinated with a world-view which, in effect, provided a rationale for moral radicalism in its very effort to establish moral order. The men who taught this course wanted to ensure stability amidst social change; but they provided no way to maintain the former or direct the latter. The academic moralists offered as absolute norms unrealizable imperatives—imperatives which, when directed at fallible men in an amoral society, were likely to become either lifeless platitudes or unrelenting war cries.

This, then, was the mental world that produced the textbooks on moral philosophy. It was a world of many ironies. The academic moralists sought to defend tradition with the tools of innovation. They sought to preserve age-old moral values in a social and intellectual order uncongenial to those values. They used the logic and the language of a new ethics to express what was essentially a religious meaning that could not be so expressed. The philosophical creed of the American academicians contained a parenthetical assumption that was to produce unforeseen consequences:

> I believe in the authority of Scripture, no less than sound philosophy (always in harmony,) . . .[12]

Man's Moral Nature

4

The Legacy of the Scottish Enlightenment

The study of morals, John Witherspoon once said, must begin with the study of man. "It seems a point agreed upon, that the principles of duty and obligation must be drawn from the nature of man. That is to say, if we can discover how his Maker formed him, or for what he intended him, that certainly is what he ought to be."[1] Witherspoon, president of what is today Princeton University, was born in Scotland in 1723 and trained at the University of Edinburgh. He spoke in the Scottish tradition of philosophy. What man ought to be depends on what he is; and what man is can be discovered by an empirical study of the human mind. American academic moralists of the mid-nineteenth century shared this assumption, and therefore emphasized the relation between mental science and moral philosophy. The science of mind provided the first clue to the science of duty.[2]

The American textbooks on moral philosophy presented ethical theories that were eclectic, borowing in varying proportions not only from Scottish common-sense philosophy but also from English empiricism, French eclecticism, and German idealism. It would thus be a mistake to regard academic philosophy in mid-nineteenth-century America as dominated by the Scottish school.[3] Still, the Scottish philosophers warrant special attention because, in their ingenious use both of logical and of psychological methods to support metaphysical claims and ethical judgments, the Scots represent a philosophical point of view that influenced all the writers whom we are considering. Francis Bowen and Noah Porter, for instance, who later in their careers incorporated a good deal of German idealism into their philosophies, had been early champions of the no-nonsense empiricism of the Scottish philosophers. The Scots, Porter once observed, enter the temple of philosophy through the only appropriate vestibule, that of psychology; and it is to them that we must turn if we wish to close the gap between "mind" and "reality."[4]

James McCosh, in his compendious history of the Scottish philosophy, picked Francis Hutcheson (1694–1746) as the founder of the school. Although Hutcheson was born in Northern Ireland, he was of Scottish descent and was educated at the University of Glasgow, where he was to serve as professor of moral philosophy from 1730 to 1746. He had been influenced by John Locke and by Locke's pupil, the third earl of Shaftesbury, and, like them, followed an inductive approach in the study of the mind. Although Hutcheson agreed with Locke that we possess no innate ideas, he nevertheless insisted that we are born with certain psychological capabilities that develop as we mature. According to McCosh, Hutcheson "gave the modern stimulus to philosophical speculation in Scotland" by using the empirical, introspective technique to discover "certain cognitive powers . . . in our very nature" which "operate independent of any notice we may take of them."[5] The quality of our experience and thought, Hutcheson believed, is partly determined by our mental constitution. Hutcheson was mainly interested in explaining our moral and aesthetic judgments, which he traced to the sentiments, and which, he insisted, are spontaneous and not derived from any calculation of self-interest or usefulness.[6] David Hume, Adam Smith, and many other eighteenth-century philosophers were much influenced by Hutcheson, and he was widely admired for disengaging morality from selfish or prudential considerations, insisting as he did that virtue consists in disinterested benevolence. But some criticized him for separating, at least in his earlier writings, the "moral sense" from the reason, thereby removing morality from the realm of rational argument and encouraging ethical subjectivism. Hutcheson was on the right track in his empirical and psychological approach to philosophical questions, it was agreed. But he erred by apparently abandoning the quest for a universal basis of moral and metaphysical authority.[7]

By the nineteenth century American thinkers were looking not to Hutcheson but to later Scottish philosophers for their inspiration—to men like Thomas Reid (1710–96), who was generally regarded as, if not the founder, then "the fit representative of the Scottish philosophy;"[8] James Beattie (1735–1803), Reid's pungent popularizer; and Dugald Stewart (1753–1828), the great systematizer. It was, indeed, Reid and Stewart whom Emerson picked out for special praise in his undergraduate essay "Ethical Philosophy" in 1821.[9] Like Hutcheson, Reid and his followers were influenced by Lockean empiricism, although these later philosophers were concerned with the wider ramifications of the Lockean philosophy, in epistemology as well as in ethics. In the mind of Reid, empiricists like Locke and Hume had placed the entire philosophical enterprise in jeopardy by suggesting that we "know" things, outside our own subjective experience, only indirectly, through a medium of mental phantasms called "ideas." We live like men confined, as Locke put it, in a "dark room," completely dependent for our knowledge of the real world on messages mysteriously received from without. To be sure, Locke had insisted that these messages are not "fictions of our fancies" but reliable reports, but Hume had known better. Our feeling of certainty about matters of fact, Hume had said, applying Hutcheson's theory to the problem of knowledge as well as to the question of morals, is based on emotion rather than reason; and truth, as a correspondence between ideas and reality, is little more than an act of faith. We "must follow our taste and sentiment" not only in music and poetry, Hume concluded, "but likewise in philosophy."[10]

Now, neither Locke nor Hume was really suggesting that we may be imagining everything, that the tables and trees we see daily may not really exist. Rather, they were asking, how do we know when we really know something? And Hume came to the conclusion that, on strictly empirical grounds, without assuming or postulating something in advance, we cannot offer a rational answer to such a question. To put it another way, Hume discovered that the empirical method of philosophy—the method of observation—could not establish the first truths of philosophy. He who would be a consistent empiricist must remain metaphysically modest, and abandon the effort to describe the "reality" that supposedly lurks beyond his immediate experience. From this it follows that the empiricist must confine himself to ordering and describing the facts at hand, and no longer try to map out the four corners of the universe.

Thomas Reid and his followers realized that such a conclusion could have dire consequences not only for philosophy but for western culture generally. Eighteenth-century thinkers were, after all, much attracted by the empirical method, which was the method of science. And the method of science was quickly becoming the model for rational explanation. But western man had traditionally assumed that matters of religion and morality could be dealt with rationally, that faith and duty were not based on sentiment and authority alone, but also on reason and understanding. If, then, it were granted that empirical reasoning precludes us from treating the fundamental truths of philosophy and religion, man would be in a "dark room" indeed—cut off not from the world of commonplace things but from all that is holy and good. There would no longer be a rational connection between human experience and all that transcends it.

When Reid published his *Inquiry into the Human Mind, on the Principles of Common Sense* in 1764, attempting to "justify the common sense and reason of mankind" against the "skeptical subtleties" of philosophers like Hume, he had the choice either of rejecting empiricism altogether or of accepting its basic methods and assumptions while arguing that Hume's sceptical conclusions need not follow from them. He chose the latter course. Reid and his followers were committed, no less than Hume, to the new empirical and psychological approach to epistemology. The "way of observation and experiment," Reid began, is the only acceptable way to study nature, including human nature and the human mind. We study the body by studying its anatomy; and only through "an anatomy of mind" can we "discover its powers and principles."[11] Reid would use Hume's techniques to refute Hume's arguments. He would establish the first truths of religion and philosophy in an empirical, non-metaphysical way.

Reid's own epistemological position need not long detain us.[12] Essentially, he argued that the theory of ideas is at the root of the empiricist's difficulty, and that knowledge begins, not with Lockean "ideas," but with judgmental "perceptions" in which, prior to all reasoning, our sensations are registered, sorted out, and placed in a meaningful context of experience. In other words, knowledge is of a piece; it is not a disorderly collection of mental particles. We first "know" the truth of propositions. We know meanings and totalities, not disparate sense-data.[13] Reid argued that the perceptions that form the basis of knowledge are "a part of the furniture which nature hath given to the human understanding. . . . They are part of our constitution, and all the discoveries of our reason are grounded upon them. They make up what is called *the common sense of mankind*."[14]

In a way, Reid's insight was penetrating. The Lockean account of knowledge, as a collection of mental elements variously combined, was a misleading abstraction. But Reid and his followers were sometimes led to confuse matters of fact with matters of logic, of value, and of faith; and there was always the temptation to overextend oneself in claims to certainty. The affirmation of faith offered by James Beattie, Reid's disciple, illustrates the danger:

> On hearing these propositions: I exist,—Things equal to one and the same thing are equal to one another,—the sun rose to-day,—There is a God,—Ingratitude ought to be blamed and punished,—The three angles of a triangle are equal to two right angles, &c.—I am conscious that my mind readily

39

admits and acquiesces in them. I say, that I believe them to be true; that is, I conceive them to express something conformable to the nature of things.[15]

Common sense avoids the idols of the cave, Henry Sidgwick once remarked, but what of the idols of the tribe?

Confident that the "common sense of mankind" was unassailable, and at times confusing what we habitually take for granted with what we really know, the Scottish philosophers addressed themselves to the question of morality. To them, sceptical philosophers like Hume were dangerous to society, disturbers of the moral peace. Scepticism, Beattie cautioned, is not "confined to points of mere speculation, but has been extended to practical truths of the highest importance, even to the principles of morality and religion."[16] To overcome such scepticism, the Scottish philosophers attempted to show both that human nature is moral and that man is capable of knowing certain fundamental moral truths. In doing this, they were particularly indebted to two prominent British moralists, Joseph Butler and Richard Price.

Like Butler, and of course Francis Hutcheson, Thomas Reid grounded moral judgment in human nature.[17] According to Butler, human nature is something like a miniature society, constituted by God and governed by the "conscience" or "moral sense," which has supervisory authority over all our powers and faculties. The conscience is, as it were, the "rule of right" within our being. (It was this added note of moral authority that made Butler's conception of the moral sense superior to Hutcheson's earlier description.) Following Butler's lead, Reid maintained that the conscience both distinguishes right from wrong and inspires moral emotions to attend its judgments, approving our virtues and scolding us for our wickedness.[18] Conscience, in performing these functions, reveals "the intention of nature." The conscientious man acts naturally, hence in obedience to God. A man's conscience is, in fact, "the law of God written in his heart." It restricts him, in the exercise of his powers, to his proper (natural) limits; and it guides him, in his active life, toward his natural (divinely appointed) ends.[19] Man, considered in his entirety, is by nature a moral being.

Our moral judgments, Reid insisted, are not simply the product of our subjective experience. Rather, moral judgments are based on our intellectual apprehension of some objective truth. Moral judgment is "a rational principle of action grounded upon our constitution as rational creatures."[20] In asserting this, Reid was joining the moral psychology of Butler and Hutcheson with the rationalistic ethics of Richard Price.[21] Building on Price's theory, Reid pointed out that the "reason" involved in moral judgment is not a discursive but an immediate and intuitive process, prior to all "reasoning." The dictates of the conscience, in other words, are just as fundamental and self-authenticating as other common-sense dictates, and have to be trusted, like the testimony of our eyes in the study of astronomy, to provide the "first principles of morals, whose truth is immediately perceived without reasoning."[22]

Although, as certain critics have pointed out, Reid was somewhat too quick to extend the analogy between ordinary empirical statements of fact and specific moral judgments, and often confused moral objectivity with moral certainty,[23] he had nonetheless achieved a remarkable synthesis of the psychological and the objectivist approaches to ethics. In Reid's hands the study of morals did, indeed, seem like a science. The question of moral values was to be approached as one approaches a matter of fact. And the question of ultimate ends was to be answered rationally, not in the optative but in the indicative mood.

Reid's moral theory was elaborated by his follower, Dugald Stewart, in 1828. Stewart stressed the moral nature of man and the rationality of moral judgments.[24] He also pointed out the practical importance of offering "academical instruction" in ethical theory in order to put an end to philosophical doubt and, thereby, to promote public and private virtue.[25] Stewart's long and tiresome discussion of the "active powers of man," cut down to size in the abridgement published by James Walker in 1849, went through nine American editions by 1866.[26] Directly or indirectly, the

Scottish synthesis of rational ethics and what Henry Sidgwick calls "moral psychology" was to have considerable influence on moral philosophy in the United States, just as the Scottish common-sense philosophy in general influenced many other areas of American thought.[27]

The Scottish synthesis seemed urgently needed in the early nineteenth century. Public order demanded sound morality; and sound morality depended on wholesome convictions. A decisive restatement and defense of the first truths of philosophy would secure faith, ensure morality, and preserve order. Many thinking persons, bewildered by the rapid changes taking place around them, looked to the Scottish common-sense philosophers for a reappearance of philosophical sanity. That the Scottish philosophy was widely appealing does not mean, however, that its formulations and solutions were always accepted wholesale. It was, rather, that the Scottish *approach* to philosophy—its resolute good sense, its avoidance of abstruse speculations, its straightforward moralizing—appealed to ordinary people's common experience and practical judgment, to conventional wisdom. For many, the Scots had shown the way a public philosophy, a philosophy not of the closet but of the schoolroom and, it was hoped, of the marketplace, should be written.

Although American academic moralists drew freely on other sources in addition to the Scottish common-sense philosophy, they followed the Scots in their dual allegiance to empiricism, including the "science" of the mind, and to rationalism. Believing that Reid and his followers had not gone far enough, however, the American moralists were generally more insistent than were the Scots that the moral reality of which they spoke, the basis of moral authority, was really real—that the universe was truly governed by a just god according to the dictates of moral law. Conscience, supplemented by revelation, was to bridge the epistemological gap between man's mind and the moral law. Will, aided by the grace of God, was to conform the secret heart to the transcendent standard of right.

5

Conscience

The progress of ethics from the late seventeenth to the early nineteenth century, said G. Stanley Hall, "was the tediously controversial transition from the view that morality was a code of laws which God revealed in Scripture, to the view that his code was best studied in the innate intuitions and sentiments of man."[1] This description strikes at the heart of the matter. The American academic moralists believed that human nature is moral, and that man's moral nature is somehow in tune with a moral order of things. Such a belief was important to men who, wishing to uphold God's immutable "code of laws," were faced with the secularization of ethics, varying interpretations of the meaning of Scripture, and an increasingly sophisticated examination of the nature of moral obligation. Conscience became a crucial link between man and moral reality, somehow providing reliable knowledge of our moral duties.

The academic moralists began by insisting, as Thomas Reid had done, that mind and body, spirit and matter, are distinct. This insistence preserved the Christian soul, avoiding the dangers of the mind-matter analogy—materialism, necessitarianism, "sentimentalism," and hedonism. The mind is not inert. It is not like a lump of soft wax, passively receiving impressions from the outside; nor are our volitions like the forced motions of a billiard ball. The separation of mind and matter not only preserved the former's inward vitality: it also provided a methodological rationale for a psychology based on introspection. Only mind is equipped to study mind, and consciousness is at once the field and the instrument of investigation. A psychologized philosophy made it possible to satisfy the demands of empiricism, while at the same time restoring order to matters of ultimate concern that had once been the subject of philosophical strife.[2]

The battle for ethical certainty was now half won. Introspection showed that man has a moral constitution. By refusing to explain the functions of mind by an analogy to matter, the academic moralists were able to apply a reverse analogy. Mind is not part of the material order, but is it not apparent that the material universe is part of a *moral* order? These philosophers could assume the methodological rigor of the physical sciences, and at the same time preserve moral values, simply by describing human "nature" as moral before they drew the analogy between human nature and nature in general.[3] The analogy solved, or seemed to solve, the question of the epistemology of morals. How do we know the right? By consulting our own minds. How do we know that the mind tells us what is truly and objectively right? Because of the remarkable correspondence between mind and moral reality. Such reasoning as this is the extension and application of the analogical technique used so successfully by Joseph Butler in his argument against deism. Butler had begun by arguing, as Leslie Stephen puts it, that man is intelligible only "as a fraction, not as an integer," in a moral universe. Therefore, what we know about man can, by analogy, be used to explain moral and spiritual matters that are in themselves beyond our knowing.[4]

Francis Wayland, who took pains to acknowledge Butler as "the author to whom I am under the greatest obligation," relied heavily both on Butler's theory of the conscience and on his analogical technique.[5] According to Wayland, the conscience is an authoritative power of inner surveillance that functions in harmony with an objective moral order of things. There are objective moral "relations" among persons that are discerned by the intellect (that God is our benefactor, for example), and with reference to which our intentions to act one way or another assume a "moral quality."

The conscience, by discovering this moral quality, makes us "conscious of the obligations arising from these relations," informing us, for instance, that we owe our benefactor a debt of gratitude. Wayland was anxious to show that the conscience tells us something true, that its dictates correspond with some objective reality. There is, he said, "a world without us and a world within us, which exactly correspond to each other." By divine contrivance, there is "light without, and the eye within; beauty without, and taste within; moral qualities without, and conscience to judge them."[6] This correspondence, established analogically rather than logically, was, for Wayland, as basic to morals as it was to epistemology.

Wayland described the conscience as a single and unique "faculty," or mental power; but he was willing to concede that its function could be performed by several faculties interacting.[7] He was concerned only to show that there is in human activity a moral quality that men can perceive. Whatever its precise nature, conscience performs three kinds of operations, intellectual, emotional, and sensual. It discriminates between right and wrong; it evokes a feeling of obligation that prompts us to act rightly; and it causes us pleasure or pain when we behave well or wickedly.[8] The first, "discriminating," function is crucial in the epistemology of morals. Wayland distinguishes this function from mere sensation, from emotion, and from discursive reasoning. Reasoning, for example, discloses the various relations in which we stand with respect to others, and shows us the most efficient means of performing our duties; but only the conscience makes us aware of the unique "moral quality," the ethical significance, of these relations, thus establishing obligation. This insight comes in the form of "intuitions" or "original suggestions of the intellect," such as our ideas of causation or duration.[9] When we realize that a judge has knowingly condemned an innocent man to death, the "idea of wrong arises unbidden within us." Our ideas of right and wrong are

not derived from reasoning. They are the necessary result of no previous mental state. There is nothing that intervenes between cognition of the act and the spontaneous existence of the moral idea.[10]

Our moral ideas, antecedent to reasoning, are part of the very structure of our rational experience.

At this point Wayland introduced a complication. He knew that the conscience is fallible, that what we believe to be right is not always so. It is necessary, therefore, to consult the "moral law," according to which righteous conduct is rewarded and wicked conduct is punished, and to seek the "additional light" offered in Scripture and "natural religion." In other words, we must try to learn what God wants us to do; for God's knowledge of right and wrong is perfect, whereas man's is only partial. To supplement the judgments of the conscience, we may, for example, turn to natural religion, a method of ethical reasoning premised on the belief that God wills the happiness of mankind, and that what promotes human happiness must conform to God's will and, therefore, be right. Wayland thus modified his intuitionist ethics with a version of theological utilitarianism.[11]

This modification was necessary in view of the fact that actual right and wrong, as distinct from what conscientious but fallible man might mistakenly think them to be, depend "upon the relations under which we are created and the obligations resulting from them, and are in their nature immutable."[12] These "relations," however, are ascertained intellectually, not intuitively. And we act intellectually, exercising our discursive reason, when we consult Scripture, natural religion, or "moral law." As far as ethical knowledge is concerned, in fact, the moral intuition is needed only to show us that certain moral relations impose *prima-facie* obligations. By this time, however, intuition seems superfluous. Given our commitment to obey God and to conform to his moral government of things, we already have enough "additional light" to transact the ethical business of life. In his effort to join an intuitionist moral psychology with a faith in an eternal, transcendent moral code, Wayland violated the principle of parsimony.

Wayland merits our attention because he exhibits the

concerns and some of the confusions of the academic moralists. He tried to do at least three things. He wanted to account for moral obligation without recourse to the selfish theory held by Paley. He hoped to answer the question of the epistemology of morals: how do we arrive at the conviction that we are morally obligated to do something? Finally, he attempted to make the metaphysical argument that there are certain transcendent and immutable moral standards that are eternally valid irrespective of human judgment or opinion. His discussion of the "moral quality" of actions reflects the first concern. His treatment of "moral relations" and "moral law" reflects the third concern. But his theory of conscience reflects not only his second, epistemological, concern but his concerns about obligation and moral standards as well. Such a combination was likely to cause confusion.

The academic moralists were in general agreement in what may be called their moral realism—their conviction that man is capable of knowing the first truths of morals and that these first truths have some kind of independent ontological status. All spoke of the conscience, although they disagreed on its precise nature and function. All insisted that the conscience is, in moral epistemology, a rational (but not necessarily intuitive) faculty or process, that our moral judgments are products of the reason and not of the emotions, although they may be attended by such emotions as approval or disapprobation. All insisted that the conscience should command our desires and interests, and that no consideration "arising from the love of pleasure or the fear of pain, nay, that no consideration arising from the consequences either to ourselves or to others, should come into competition with it."[13] But all realized that the conscience is fallible, at least in specific judgments, and therefore has to be cultivated and properly educated. And all insisted that the conscience, however defined, furnishes some sort of ethical truth: that is, the conscience informs man about the moral universe just as the senses and the understanding inform him about the physical universe.

There was division over the exact nature of the conscience. Is the conscience a separate faculty, distinct from every other, offering entirely original information? Or is "conscience" merely a convenient term to describe a certain kind of rational operation? The academic moralists were about evenly split over this question, although the split was not really fundamental, as witness Wayland's remark that moral obligation is little affected whether it be disclosed by one or by several powers of the mind.[14] The disagreement among the academicians over the precise function of the conscience was more significant. What epistemological task does the conscience—unique faculty or not—perform? Some, such as Mark Hopkins, had no need of a theory of conscience at all, since their moral system was not based on moral intuition but on a calculation of the greatest good. Nevertheless, even though Hopkins appropriately denied that the conscience is a unique faculty, he still spoke of it as "the proclamation within us of the moral law," which "intuitively" affirms our obligation to choose the supreme good as our ultimate end, and which "judges" the "moral quality" of actions.[15] Others whose teleological moral theory resembled Hopkins's, among them Charles G. Finney and even Noah Porter, who emphatically rejected intuitionism, relied on the conscience to fill the gaps in their ethical epistemology.[16] For these men the conscience was not necessary to distinguish right from wrong or to establish moral obligation, since these matters were presumably settled elsewhere in their theories. Many admitted this. Yet they ascribed to the conscience an epistemological as well as a hortatory and coercive function. Why? It seems that the conscience, even when stripped of its intuitive powers, still suggested authority, still implied a connection between man's mind and the moral order of things.

At the other end of the theoretical spectrum, Wayland and many of those who elaborated intuitionist theories entertained doubts about the idea of the conscience. The crux seems to lie in the question whether the conscience proposes general moral principles or rules, or judges individual acts. Asa Mahan, who knew his Kant, was probably the most consistent of the intuitionists in insisting that the conscience is concerned only with formal, universal principles.[17] The others argued either that our moral intuition judges only actions or, more commonly and rather confusedly, that it both delivers the "first principles" of morals and also judges specific actions.[18] In either case the question arises, by what standard is one to determine whether one's specific intuitive judgment of an action is correct? The question was a troubling one. If everything men believed to be right *were* right, said Archibald Alexander, opinion would be law, false religion would be true, and morals would be purely a matter of personal preference. Obviously, he maintained, there is a standard of absolute right to which any human intuition is an approximation.[19] We judge the closeness of the approximation not by another intuition, which could only offer another approximation, but by the discursive reason applied to Scripture and experience. We seek a higher law that exists beyond our intuitions. If we say this, however, what essential epistemological purpose does the conscience serve?

As an epistemological device, the conscience was in some cases superfluous, in most cases unreliable, and in any case dangerous—inviting both subjectivism and fanaticism. Yet the conscience was a practical and psychological necessity for men seeking to find the key to eternity in the study of man. In the final analysis, the academic moralists were not primarily concerned with the nature of moral judgments, nor with how we come to regard a certain course of action as our duty. Their real concern was to re-establish the connection between man and God's law. And this connection need not be a strictly logical one—for the law of God is directed at man as a totality, and not only at his reason. Conscience may not be entirely reliable as a vehicle of moral knowledge, Wayland admitted, but it remains the "most authoritative impulse" to which we are susceptible.[20] God, said Alexander, "has not left himself without a witness, in the breast of every man."[21]

Conscience is our inborn assent to God's moral authority over us, the testimony in our heart and mind of our subservience. Viewed in this light, it is not difficult to understand why, in their textbooks, the academic moralists, no matter which ethical theory they subscribed to, were so ready to compare our moral judgments with sense perceptions, and so easily spoke of the conscience as "admonishing" and "instructing" us in almost every action. They wanted to impart to their students a deep feeling both of the immediacy of God's moral law and of the sure truth of fundamental moral principles. The theory of conscience seemed to serve well in both these departments. The sense of immediacy is achieved as God's law becomes an inward law, and, as Francis Bowen put it, makes a Sinai of our heart.[22] And the sense of moral certainty is achieved when one reflects on the authority with which the voice of conscience speaks: the fundamental ideas furnished by the conscience are self-authenticating, and point to a reality beyond themselves. "Every fundamental idea in the human mind," said Asa Mahan with reference to the idea of rewards and punishments, "implies the actual existence of a corresponding reality." Otherwise, he added, "nature herself, in her most sacred revelations, is a lie, and nothing else."[23] The authority of its dictates makes conscience the unimpeachable witness of God's written law. James McCosh put it thus:

> It would be a great mistake to suppose that the written law could have efficacy on us without the inward faculty [conscience]; on the contrary, the former pre-supposes, and is especially addressed to the latter. For how can we be made to know or feel that we are bound to obey the written law? Plainly by the law of the heart, which says, this is right.[24]

Conscience served as the indispensable link between man and what is forever worthy of man's deepest reverence.

Recalling his experience at the University of Vermont in the 1870's, John Dewey puzzled over the "almost sacrosanct air that enveloped the idea of intuitions." Dewey was remembering the twilight of an age when ethical and religious truths seemed as obvious as empirical facts. Looking back half a century, he observed that "somehow the cause of all holy and valuable things was supposed to stand or fall with the validity of intuitionism."[25]

And perhaps it did.

6

Will

Nothing, Kant said, "nothing in the world—indeed nothing even beyond the world—can possibly be conceived which could be called good without qualification except a *good will*."[1] Once it is taken for granted that ethical truth is knowable, the problem of morality becomes a problem of will. One chooses either to perform or to shirk one's duty. In the early nineteenth century in America the will occasioned considerable ethical controversy. It was, of course, agreed that we praise or blame a moral agent for his intentions, not merely for his actions. The palsied gesture, though it injures another, draws no moral censure. But what is an intention? What constitutes an act of free will?

For the thoughtful Christian moralist, these questions raised many theological problems. The moralist and the theologian, after all, start on quite different grounds. The theologian is concerned with God and with the mysterious God-man relation, a relation that, since it is partly supernatural, is partly beyond human understanding. Moral philosophers since the seventeenth century, on the other hand, have been concerned to treat ethics independently of religion. Moreover, anxious to sharpen thought and reduce mystery, moral philosophers—in the spirit of the times—demanded a new precision in language, and sought what Thomas Sprat had called "a close, naked, natural way of speaking."[2] To accomplish this, eighteenth-century British philosophers seriously examined ordinary language, the idiom of the "vulgar," striving to clarify common usage. This process of clarification, fully as much as the new commitment to reason and to the autonomy of ethics, set theology and moral philosophy at odds with each other. The theologian, if he is to express what is ultimately ineffable, must resort to the language of paradox. The philosopher, if he is to achieve clarity and precision in thought and language, must first of all banish paradox.

The conflict between theology and moral philosophy is especially evident in the problem of will. In ordinary language, moral obligation implies ability. One cannot be morally obligated to do the impossible; one cannot be charged with an offense one is unable to avoid committing. Yet theologians, particularly those in the Calvinist tradition, would express their religious vision in terms of just such a paradox. Although John Calvin granted man virtually nothing as a moral agent, he emphasized man's terrible guilt and responsibility.[3] Before God, morally puny man is forever accountable. This affirmation is a central element of the Calvinist, as of the Pauline, world view; and its contradictoriness was evident to Christian thinkers long before the eighteenth century. But by the middle of the eighteenth century the paradoxes of theology had become more than ever difficult to maintain. Many, besides Joseph Butler, were to insist that "everything is what it is, and not another thing." And no theological alchemy could translate inability into ability.

Or could it? Jonathan Edwards was well aware of both the demands of piety and the techniques of the new philosophy when he directed his attention to the problem of the *Freedom of Will* in his famous treatise of 1754. The book is in fact less concerned with "the will" than with the "act of choosing or choice," which Edwards defines simply as becoming desirous of an available good to which one had previously been indifferent. Having become interested and found a given possibility most agreeable, we have opted for that possibility: we have "willed" something. The logic of volition ends here.[4] Edwards's discussion is almost unpleasantly taut and strictly empirical, apparently leaving further discussion of the matter to neurophysiology rather than philosophy.

Edwards is important to our discussion of academic moral philosophy not only because he expresses both theological and ethical concerns, but because his treatment of the problem of free will raised issues that were still being debated in the nineteenth century, especially by those Americans in the tradition of New England theology.[5] He had connected will to desire so tightly that, in the minds of many, he had made rational morality virtually impossible. To "will" is to do what one wants, he said; this and nothing more. What one wants is what one finds most agreeable. To speak of "free" will is redundant and confusing, for all choices motivated solely by one's desires are free. Such, indeed, is the paradigm for free choice. (Edwards was as expert in appealing to ordinary language as any thinker of his age.) Can one *want* whatever one wants? Certainly not, said Edwards. Such a question misuses language, as witness the infinite regress it implies: can one want whatever one wants to want to want?[6] The very idea of choice involves the idea of a necessary connection between desire and choice. Without this connection there is, properly speaking, no choice. A choice is free if it is made without physical restraint or force.[7]

The tightness of Edwards's reasoning expressed the terrible limitations of human existence, and his implacable logic almost serves as a metaphor for the human predicament. Man's freedom makes him his own slave, for man cannot act outside the logic of his own free action. Skillfully analyzing ordinary language, Edwards restored the language of paradox. Turning common sense upon itself, he showed that the sinner can be bound yet free—bound, in fact, by his very freedom. There can be no human or natural cure for human nature.

A fundamental difference in point of view separates Jonathan Edwards from most philosophers, even most Christian philosophers, in the mid-nineteenth century. Whereas Edwards regarded man primarily as a sinner in the hands of an angry God, the later thinkers thought of man primarily as a responsible moral agent performing the duties of a citizen in a vast moral government. Edwards, for all his logical precision, approached the soul of man with a sense of profound awe. Later Christian moralists, for all their pious rhetoric, usually thought of the soul (the mind) as the object of empirical inquiry, subject to precise analysis. Henry Tappan, who taught moral philosophy at New York University and later became president of the University of Michigan, advised philosophers not to let themselves be misled by theological "opinions." The will must be studied strictly in terms of the "laws of our being," he said. It must "be subjected to the legitimate methods of psychological investigation," not in the spirit of theology but in "the free, fearless, honest spirit of Baconian observation."[8]

New social concerns further separated American academic moralists of the mid-nineteenth century from Edwards. As public moralists in a free society it was necessary that they emphasize human freedom and responsibility in order to encourage men in the pursuit of righteousness. To stress moral inability would only provide an excuse for licentiousness. Many besides Horace Mann had observed that in a free society man's baser passions and appetites are liberated along with his higher faculties. In such a situation it would be nothing less than socially suicidal to retain a theory that denied man control over his lower instincts and desires, and hence over his actions. Man's power to do good must at least equal his capacity for mischief. The philosophy of human nature had to keep pace with the ever-increasing potential of men living in a commercial and democratic society.

The nineteenth-century Christian moralist, then, had to balance his theological commitments over against his "Baconian" spirit and his social concerns. He had to offer an account of man's moral capabilities that conflicted neither with prevailing moral and psychological theories, nor with the hortatory demands of his office, nor with his own theological persuasion concerning God's sovereignty and man's estate. To offer any account of man's moral capabilities, one had to begin with a very careful description of the will and its function.

For nineteenth-century thinkers, steeped in the psychology of Scottish common sense and French eclecticism, the noun "will" denoted a particular power of the mind, distinct both from the reason and the emotions.[9] The tripartite division of mind into rational, emotional, and volitional faculties was considered a significant improvement on the Edwardsean psychology. Edwards, it was observed, had failed to separate the will from the feelings and had thus confused choice with desire. Armed with a more useful division of the mind, Charles G. Finney expressed confidence that neither the understanding nor the emotions could ever "lord it over the will."[10] This new analysis of the human mind at once raised man from the status of mere sinner to that of a fully functioning moral agent, and made explicit what had once been ambiguous and fundamentally mysterious—the act of choice.

Once he had accepted the psychological approach to morals, with its precise analysis of man's moral powers, even the most dedicated Calvinist might be expected to have difficulty maintaining his orthodoxy. Calvin himself, although he had grudgingly accepted the faculty psychology of the ancient Greeks, had insisted that the "heathen philosophers" could offer only an inadequate psychology "because they sought for a complete edifice among ruins, and for beautiful order in the midst of confusion."[11] There can be no naturalistic psychology, Calvin believed, because the human soul has been damaged beyond recognition. So Archibald Alexander, one of the staunchest of the staunch Old School Presbyterians, attempted a truly difficult feat when he tried to combine a Calvinist assessment of man's depravity with his own moral theory.

If there is to be moral responsibility, said Alexander, there must be moral agency; that is, man must have a "self-determining power" over his actions.[12] Our morally significant actions depend on our volitions; and our volitions, Alexander maintained in the tradition of Edwards, "are invariably determined by the strongest desire."[13] Alexander did not follow Edwards completely, however. He distinguished between such "rational" desires as the desire to perform one's duty and those associated with our appetites and passions. He regarded the rational and emotional "desires" as contending impulses, the strongest of which would prevail. As it turned out, however, his distinction between kinds of desire really meant little, because he maintained that all our desires may be good or evil in themselves, regardless of whether they are acted upon or not. For all of them reflect a "hidden disposition"—a central part of our character—which is itself good or evil, and is accordingly the proper object of moral judgment. Our hidden disposition is the original source of our desires, our volitions, and our actions.[14]

The question now arises whether man has a "self-determining power" over his "hidden disposition." Alexander did not satisfactorily treat this question, and the reason is clear. Either man lacks the ability to alter his hidden disposition—in which case Alexander would be implying that there can be moral responsibility without moral agency, thus contradicting himself—or man has the ability (along with the duty) to alter his hidden disposition, in which case Alexander would be, theologically, moving in the direction of Pelagianism and even perfectionism.

The distinction between the moral philosopher and the Calvinist theologian becomes evident. Moral philosophy is concerned with man's actual attributes as a moral being. If all men, through some "hidden disposition," are accomplices in original sin—as Alexander was really suggesting—then sin becomes a common denominator in human nature and cancels out of the human equation as far as moral obligation is concerned. If, on the other hand, grace is a real possibility for all men, it is not functionally different from any other moral endowment; and the important theological distinction between nature and grace is jeopardized. Ethical theory, to be universally applicable, could neither discriminate between the regenerate and the unregenerate nor tolerate the uncertainty of divine election. And the new moral psychology, in its precise description of man's moral nature, could not take account of the unpredictable and arbitrary intrusions of God's grace.

Because he was an orthodox Calvinist of the Old School, Alexander is theologically atypical of the textbook moralists.

Nevertheless, he serves as an example in two respects. In the first place, he represents a concern of all the academic moralists—whether they happened to be moderate Calvinists like Francis Wayland, crypto-Pelagians like Finney, or Unitarians like James Walker—that their description of man's moral nature should acknowledge the sinner's need for God's help. That is, regardless of their doctrinal positions, all of them wanted to make the grace of God a factor in their moral psychology, while at the same time they insisted on man's moral responsibility.[15] "We tremble equally," said James McCosh, a moderate Calvinist, "at the idea of removing the creature from under the control of God, and of making him so dependent as to involve God in the responsibility for his acts."[16] Yet almost in spite of themselves, and despite the doctrinal divisions among them, these academicians—Alexander included—show the movement of American thought in the mid-nineteenth century away from theological mystery and toward philosophical common sense. Speaking of moral agency, Alexander observed that "we appeal to the consciousness of every rational being. No arguments, however plausible, are of any force against intuitive first principles."[17] It was precisely this appeal to the "consciousness of every rational being" that threatened theological orthodoxies of every kind. Under the banners of "consciousness" and "intuitive first principles," American thought was moving inexorably toward free human agency, unshackling the will at whatever cost to theological doctrines, plausible or otherwise.[18]

Archibald Alexander serves as an instructive example in a second way. In tracing human actions back to a "hidden disposition," he expanded his view of the act of will in a manner characteristic of the academic moralists. It was clear that motives and desires profoundly influence choice, whether they determine it or not. It was no less clear to educators that a man's basic character makes him more susceptible to some motives than to others, and that his character is shaped by his values and ideals. It may be said, therefore, that in some measure men determine their character, and hence their conduct in life, by their choice of allegiances. As

Jonathan Edwards himself had put it, there are ultimate acts of will as well as limited acts of will; and the former determine the latter. The truly good man thus dedicates himself to serving the well-being of God and the universe, and from this act of dedication other, more limited, acts of benevolence follow. The miser or the lecher, on the other hand, plays a part in shaping his character by letting his mind become fixed on some base and ignoble pursuit. Implicitly or explicitly, this theme is to be found in most of the ethical texts: commitment defines character, and character directs choice.[19]

Even Francis Wayland, with his somewhat narrow focus on the "moral quality" of specific actions ("intentions"), hinted that intention may involve more than the simple design exemplified in such actions as deliberately injuring another. For, he observed, the way we exercise our imagination can affect our intentions. The "conceptions of our imagination," therefore, "may develop moral character [moral quality?]." Since the "moral character of an action resides in the intention, and as whatever tends to corrupt the intention must be wrong, the meditating with pleasure upon vice, which has manifestly this tendency, must be wrong also."[20] Our moral responsibility, Wayland was suggesting, extends beneath our immediate intentions. Purity of intention demands purity of heart. Wayland's observation was hortatory rather than analytical, based on psychological observation rather than on logical demonstration. For precisely these reasons it suggests a significant reordering of intellectual priorities.

In spite of Robert Baird's observation, in 1844, that one of the major subjects of theological debate at the time in America was "the old question of 'fate and free-will,' "[21] in the textbooks on moral philosophy, at least, the emphasis was already subtly shifting. To be sure, at Oberlin Finney and Asa Mahan still fought the good fight against Calvinist doctrine,[22] while Alexander at Princeton tried to translate the principles of Calvin and Knox into a new language. But the emphasis fell increasingly on man's moral nature broadly considered, and on the proper means of refining and elevating that nature. Jasper Adams impatiently dismissed the theoretical questions altogether. "It is the object of moral philosophy," he announced, not to belabor subtle points of doctrine, but "to investigate the moral constitution of man and the appropriate sphere of his duties."[23] The discussion of the will led the academic moralists back through intentions and motives to character and commitment, in which the incompatibility between piety and moralism did not seem so striking since character and commitment are elusive concepts that are not susceptible to the kind of precise analysis one can bring to intention and choice. The discussion now took a welcome turn. Having separated will from the emotions and appetites, having distinguished volition from simple desire, the academic moralists felt that they had given man sufficient freedom to act as a responsible moral agent. Attention was no longer centered on the logical connection of cause and effect, with which Edwards had riveted the sinner to his own depravity, nor on the troublesome relation between human nature and grace. The important thing was man's moral constitution—with all its intellectual, affective, and active powers—as something in need of proper training and instruction.[24]

In their treatment of man's moral nature, the academic moralists were finally unable either to connect conscience with objective moral truth or to offer a clear and consistent account of the limits of moral ability. Their effort failed because it was ill-conceived. It proved impossible to combine empiricism and intuitionism, psychologism and ontologism, human freedom and divine sovereignty—and to maintain intact each end of each polarity. More fundamentally, it was impossible to establish metaphysical truths by non-metaphysical means, to capture the meaning of a religious experience in a scientific formula. Modern theories cannot express ancient faiths. But, in a way, none of this mattered very much. There was never any real doubt that man had been constituted a moral being, able to know and to obey God's moral law. The confusing vagaries of theoretical ethics, as Jasper Adams observed, must not be permitted to distract the mind from the real concern—the demands of practical morals. The problem of man's moral nature was properly to be handled not through philosophy but through education, the appropriate introduction to the moral life.

59

Part III

The Virtuous Life

7

Moral Education

Higher education in mid-nineteenth-century America, as we have seen, was expected to produce an educated class capable of exerting responsible moral leadership in American society. On the continent of Europe, it was frequently observed, the educated class had responded to the collapse of feudal authority and to the speculations of the Enlightenment by challenging and undermining public faith and morals. The French revolution, its bloody aftermath, and its authoritarian resolution clearly demonstrated the disastrous results of this alienation of the intellectuals. In this country, Francis Bowen warned, the clergy and the "educated laity" must work together "to erect a barrier against the licentious and infidel speculations which are pouring upon us from Europe like a flood."[1] To produce an educated laity willing to co-operate in erecting such a barrier was a primary responsibility of the old-time college. College students, who would constitute the nation's educated class, must not only be instructed in the first principles of sound morality but also be scrupulously trained in the conscientious performance of duty. The most intensive portion of this instruction and training was received during the student's senior year, in the course in moral philosophy.

Instruction in the first principles of morality centered on the description of man's moral nature, the definition of major ethical terms, and the refutation of certain "erroneous" and "pernicious" theories of morals—including, invariably, utilitarianism. All this constituted "theoretical ethics," and was presented concisely and authoritatively, as a body of truths to be learned and accepted. The main purpose served by theoretical ethics, aside from clarification and definition, was to establish the fact that our moral responsibility is a matter of objective moral law that is rationally apprehensible; and that moral duty is not based on mere sentiment, subjective whim, or selfish design. For only if the certainty and authority of morals were established, clearly and decisively, could moral philosophy perform its second and most important function: that of training college students in the actual performance of duty.

One's duties begin at one's own doorstep. That is, the law of obligation comprehends not only one's relation with others but one's self-development as well. Higher education, insofar as it was concerned with self-development, acquainted the student with two kinds of obligation to himself. First, there were duties of "natural" self-improvement, duties to develop one's natural abilities and to become a fully functioning person. Second, there were duties of "moral" self-improvement, revolving around the obligation to use one's natural abilities to perfect one's moral character. These two kinds of "duties to oneself" or "subjective duties," as they were frequently labeled, merit our attention because they are central to the concept of moral education.

Happiness is the immediate end of the first class of personal duties, those involving natural self-improvement. Happiness is not merely the satisfaction of one's appetites and desires, but the result of self-control and of a sensible concern for one's health and physical and mental development. Such prudential self-regard is both permissible and obligatory, insofar as it furthers and does not obstruct one's performance of other, higher duties. Mark Hopkins offered the most elaborate formulation of this line of reasoning in his famous "law of limitation," which described a hierarchy of drives and satisfactions according to which our "lower" impulses support and are subservient to our "higher" powers. Thus, said Hopkins, the satisfaction of one's natural appetites is morally right until it interferes with the cultivation of one's higher, intellectual powers; and further, a person's intellectual pursuits should not cause him to neglect his moral development.[2] In the tradition of Joseph Butler, most of the writers of ethical textbooks agreed that man's natural powers are basically trustworthy—at least as far as the aims of ethical education are concerned. Each power or faculty, physical and mental, was presumed to have its proper sphere; and man, it was supposed, is regulated by conscience just as nature is regulated by natural law, except that man's obedience to the dictates of conscience is volitional. Hopkins's law of limitation, which was merely a systematic elaboration of this theory, accorded with the general thinking of American academic moralists.[3] To an age still enchanted with the Newtonian world-picture, this description of the human situation as a kind of moral analogue of the cosmic order held obvious appeal. Hopkins was in fact claiming nothing more than a divinely appointed limit to all human satisfactions, rejecting self-neglect at one extreme and self-indulgence at the other.

Natural self-improvement, as the academic moralists described it in their lectures and textbooks, included specific duties to oneself. These were frequently classified as duties of self-preservation, including a proper care for one's health, with various strictures against alcohol and other drugs; duties of self-culture, including all intellectual development; and duties of self-control, especially the formation of good habits. Altogether, it was a predictable plea for a sound mind in a sound body. The treatment of natural self-improvement was designed to discourage the libertine and the voluptuary, and offered no encouragement at all to acquisitiveness, self-assertiveness, or rebelliousness.[4]

The second class of personal duties was moral self-improvement, the duty to cultivate one's good character. Of the three functions of college education, said Edward Everett of Harvard in 1846—the acquisition of knowledge, the "discipline" of the mental faculties, and the formation of good character—the last is most important. Character, said James Walker, Everett's colleague, includes both habits and the moulding of these habits "into *a consistent and harmonious whole*."[5] The consistency and harmony of this whole was crucial: good character meant integrity, the perfect and harmonious interaction of all one's mental and moral powers.

The development of sound moral character involved both training and commitment. In childhood a person's character was largely in the hands of his parents and Sunday-school teachers. Later, the custodianship was turned over to the college and its president, who stood *in loco parentis*.[6] In this respect, the course in moral philosophy, as a culmination of college training, had an important function. Judging from the textbooks, the course seems to have been designed to draw together all the scrambled admonitions and reprimands that had theretofore been lavished on a youth, to arrange them in a systematic body, and offer them as the moral legacy of the ages to be studied, cherished, and, presumably, obeyed throughout life. Besides the course in moral philosophy, the college offered a régime of strict discipline to facilitate character-training. A good college education, said Stephen Olin, president of Wesleyan University and a leading spokesman for higher education, goes beyond the narrow concern for intellectual growth, and provides the "plastic, ductile, impressible nature" of youth with most of the elements of good character through its disciplinary system. The rules and regulations of the college, for example, serve as an indispensable tool in the proper formation of the boy's character, producing such good habits as punctuality, dutifulness, honesty, and orderliness, which would become almost second nature as the years went by.[7] An educational reformer like Asa Mahan might argue that self-discipline should begin in college, and that the college should not impose arbitrary rules on students;[8] but for both Mahan and Olin the ultimate goal was the same, the formation of the man who is self-regulating and inner-directed.

The rigorous disciplining of the mind associated with college character-training reflected the premises of the faculty psychology. The various faculties of mind, grouped under reason, the emotions, and will, were thought to be, like muscles, susceptible of improvement through exercise.[9] Character was considered the controlling center of a "disciplined," "symmetrical," and "harmonious" development of the faculties, symmetry and harmony being no less important to moral educators than discipline, and all three being vital to the proper development of the "whole man."[10] The faculty psychology allowed the academic moralists, on paper at least, to take the mind apart, study it, and reassemble it as a symmetrical whole designed to function in harmony with the moral universe.

Commitment as well as training was considered essential to the formation of sound moral character; most specifically, it meant Christian faith, which was regarded as a necessary basis for morality. Without God, said Mark Hopkins, the conscience is like "an eye without light."[11] In the more evangelically oriented colleges, conversion was considered essential for good character.[12] But in all the antebellum colleges "sound moral character" was equated with Christian character. Commitment, however, implied more than Christian belief. For Charles G. Finney, writing in the tradition of Jonathan Edwards, commitment meant living in total consecration to the highest good of all being.[13] And each of the academic moralists sought to make the various moral values —honesty, chastity, respect for property—intensely personal goals, subjects of profound attachment in their students' lives. If the moral law of God is not literally inscribed within the heart, the moralist must inscribe it there himself. Moral commitment will compensate for any lingering doubts about moral truths and first principles. Exhortation is the remedy for doubt, and well-intentioned resolution is the answer to moral inability.

Glancing through the labored discussions of self-improvement and character-building in the old textbooks, the modern reader is inclined to dismiss the admonitions therein as trite and platitudinous (which they are), perhaps losing sight of the age to which this instruction was addressed. The Victorian period in America, no less than in England, was characterized by a serious concern with the quality of one's personal experience and the cultivation of wholesome habits. It is commonplace, and certainly valid, to speak of education as replacing external authority in this period, of self-control being called on to substitute for institutional controls. But we must not lead ourselves into thinking that the character-education idea was a kind of stratagem used by conservative and fearful educators to make the population obedient and docile. Training in self-mastery was not merely a device for social manipulation. The nineteenth century was a hortative age. Any "Memoir" of a nineteenth-century figure, the kind of biographical compilation customarily published by a person's heirs after his death, was usually careful to show how the man's character developed and how, by painstaking effort, he cultivated good habits and overcame bad ones. This was meant not only to inspire and instruct the reader but also to establish the moral identity of the subject, to illustrate, as it were, his secular growth in grace. What to the modern reader may seem like gratuitous moral advice appears not only in ethical textbooks but in novels, essays, and even scientific treatises throughout the century. William James, whose mind indisputably belongs to the twentieth century in many ways, was a Victorian in his moralizing tendency. His discussion of habit in the *Principles of Psychology* (1890), for instance, draws important moral lessons from a technical analysis, warning the reader to beware of "excessive novel-reading and theatre-going," lest he become a dreamy sentimentalist "who never does a manly concrete deed." And James offers as a "practical maxim" for cultivating proper "habits of the will" the admonition:

> *Keep the faculty of effort alive in you by a little gratuitous exercise every day.* That is, be systematically ascetic or heroic in little unnecessary points, do every day or two something for no reason than that you would rather not do it, so that when the hour of dire need draws nigh, it may find you not unnerved and untrained to stand the test.[14]

The nineteenth century took character-building as seriously as it did everything else. It was an age of moral pedagogy. And in this context the course in moral philosophy clearly served a purpose. The moral man, having been indoctrinated with the highest moral principles during his college years, was expected to enter society, there to continue to pursue the life of virtue, and to put his enlightened conscience in his nation's service.

8

The Performance of Duty

To guide the moral man in his lifelong pursuit of righteousness, the textbooks in moral philosophy offered a detailed listing and classification of the various moral duties—
duties not only to oneself but to others and to God as well.
Jasper Adams of Charleston College, who made something
of a study of the history of ethics and who claimed to have
bought every book on ethics "worth purchasing," observed
that this cataloguing of duties was a modern practice that
had arisen since the seventeenth century.[1] Whatever its
origins, the listing and discussion of specific duties was regarded as a highly useful aspect of ethical instruction; although one may wonder precisely what its use was, since the
usual discussion of duties was general and vague in all but
the most trifling matters. In dealing with a controversial
subject, such as slavery, the American writers were cautious,
not to say shilly-shallying.[2] In treating very general or safe
subjects, the value of thrift or the duty of forgiveness for instance, they presented platitudes as profundities, shame-
lessly labored the obvious, and exhibited, as one historian
has observed, an "almost dismaying concern with codifying
the trivialities of common-sense living."[3] This concern with
the drab intricacies of the trivial puts an almost unbridge-
able gap between the antebellum moralists and the modern
student, or perhaps any student.

Duties to oneself, or "personal duties," have been treated

71

in the preceding chapter. Not every academic moralist identified duties to oneself as a separate class. Francis Wayland, for example, spoke only of duties to others and to God. But all agreed that one is morally obligated to cultivate a good Christian character and to maintain one's mind and body in order to be able to serve others. And although Wayland did not label this a personal duty, he joined his colleagues in expressing the conviction.[4]

Duties to others, which sometimes took up as many as half the pages of the moral-philosophy textbooks, were a protean subject—including personal relations between individuals, special social relations (family or business relationships, for example), political ethics (often spilling over into the principles of government), and even issues in international law and political economy. Such diverse topics as the duty to tell the truth, filial obedience, the ethics of contracts, the evils of covetousness, duties of citizens, and the evils of slavery were all discussed under the heading "duties to others." Reserving specifically social questions for a later chapter, let us concentrate here on the questions of private duties to others—man's duties to man as man.

Although using the technical language of moral science, the American academicians usually came up with a version of the Golden Rule: "Do unto others as you would have others do unto you," perhaps adding a qualifying phrase like "in the same circumstances." Francis Wayland, for instance, divided virtue into "piety" (love of God) and "morality" (love of man). The various duties of morality, he explained, arise as one finds oneself in various "relations" that impose specific obligations: the beneficiary finds that he owes a debt of gratitude to his benefactor; the child owes his parents respect and obedience. In more general person-to-person relations, the basic duties are those of "reciprocity" and "benevolence." In examining various divisions and subdivisions of these basic duties, one finds reciprocity defined as the negative duty of not interfering with another's rights, and benevolence as the positive obligation to serve others.[5] The academic philosophers generally resembled Wayland in their division of duties into positive and negative, some, like Jasper Adams, creating a separate classification for specific Christian duties such as the duty of forgiveness.[6] These writers and teachers thus followed the lead of Joseph Butler in holding that the duties of virtue include justice as well as benevolence: a noble end cannot justify a wicked means, so one may not rob Peter in order to give alms to Paul.[7]

Duty and virtue are not equivalent. "Duty" usually refers to what is imperative and expected of a person. "Virtue," on the other hand, is often used to designate what is meritorious, what surpasses the ordinary performance of duty; and "virtue" was so used by eighteenth-century writers like Shaftesbury, who treated ethics as an appreciative discipline, in some ways analogous to aesthetics. This distinction was often blurred in the nineteenth century. Scottish moralists like Dugald Stewart regarded moral philosophy as a practical discipline intended to promote good habits in society at large.[8] In this spirit, the American textbook moralists—seeking to ennoble the average rather than to celebrate the noble—tended to join the ideals of virtue (such as saintliness) with the demands of duty (such as simple piety). They tended to obscure the distinction between the demands of duty and what goes beyond the call of duty. Given the demand for a democratic ethics, such a development is understandable, but if pushed in one direction it leads to a potentially dangerous oversimplification of complex moral issues; pushed in another, it may result in a lowered level of moral aspiration, in which simple duties are counted as the whole of virtue and humdrum moral truisms receive a spurious tone of urgency.

Wayland's discussion of the duty of veracity (painstakingly classified under Duties to Men as Men, Class One of the Duty of Reciprocity, Division First of our Duty to Others) illustrates this belaboring of the trivial. It was, and still is, considered good form for a moral philosopher to unravel the meaning of common moral injunctions in order to examine the basic principle involved. Kant, for instance, had discussed the question of veracity at some length.[9] Kant's discussion, however, was terse and to the point—always illustrative of his ethical theory. Wayland and his colleagues, on the other hand, were not simply illustrating ethical theory when they spoke of our duty to tell the truth; they were giving moral advice, as if people needed to be convinced that it is wrong to tell lies. To prove that veracity is indeed a duty, Wayland discussed our disposition to tell the truth (thus suggesting a constitutional propensity for veracity); he observed that our conscience troubles us when we lie (showing that mendacity exhibits a negative "moral quality"); he argued that man's happiness and scientific progress depend on the transmission of truth (offering a standard utilitarian argument); and, finally, he emphasized the Scriptural insistence on veracity (thus clinching the matter by evoking God's law).[10] To marshal Butlerian psychologism, Scottish intuitionism, Paleyan utilitarianism, and Biblical legalism in order to prove that it is wrong to tell lies is like using a howitzer to kill a carpet beetle. Had Wayland raised the questions of casuistry, as Kant had, dealing with cases of real moral conflict, he might have been justified. But he began with a truism ("veracity is a duty we owe to others") and never went beyond it. Wayland's students learned that honesty is a good policy, but they never learned if honesty is always the better policy.

The other academic moralists did not differ significantly from Wayland in their treatment of our duties to others—laboring the obvious and avoiding the ambiguous. The moral law of the universe, after all, unlike physical laws, governs the free conduct of intelligent beings. Hence it became the job of the old-time moralist to make the demands of the law clear and to persuade people to obey it. The times, furthermore, seemed to demand just such an extensive restatement of basic moral obligation: in an era of speculative confusion and social dislocation a clear and decisive affirmation of essential moral truths was undoubtedly comforting and reassuring. All theories, including those of ethics, may be open to question, but our moral responsibilities remain unaltered. By harping on honesty, justice, and benevolence, by drumming moral maxims into their student's heads, the academic moralists were to see to it that young people never forgot their obligations to others. One's duties to oneself boil down to something like a sound mind, a sound body, and a righteous character. One's duties to others may be as easily summarized: seek thy neighbor's best interests while respecting his fundamental rights. The precise nature of one's neighbor's "best interests" and the actual extent of his "fundamental rights" were not nearly so important as one's good intentions with respect to them.

Man's duties to God, in spite of the cosmic magnitude of the subject, received neither extensive nor profound treatment from the academic moralists. It was assumed that there is a god, that he presides over the moral government of the universe, and that men owe him various debts—including the respect and obedience due a moral governor, the gratitude due him as our creator and redeemer, and the reverence which both his office and his moral excellence command. Moreover, most of the moral philosophers maintained that our duties to God comprehend all our other duties, both to ourselves and to others. "According to the most extensive signification of the word," wrote Asa Mahan, "the term piety would include all duties of every kind."[11]

One sometimes gets the impression that the academic moralists were a little embarrassed by the discussion of duties to God. Like the Man Who Came to Dinner, God was undeniably present, he was making exorbitant demands, and he could show nothing but his universal renown to justify his claims on everybody. Joseph Haven, for instance, held an intuitionist theory of morals that made it difficult for him to offer one convincing reason why we are morally obligated to obey God at all.[12] It is next to impossible to encompass a sovereign God within a rational ethical system.[13] It seems that, their affirmations to the contrary notwithstanding, the academic moralists were not interested in constructing a strictly rational ethical theory. Moral science, like natural science, was thought to be incomplete without God. According to Mark Hopkins, the moral law is the law of love, which is the law of God.[14] Can one even construct a coherent and comprehensive moral theory without religious faith? Certainly not, Noah Porter maintained. "A materialist or atheistic philosophy must inevitably result in a superficial and inconsistent ethical system. . . ."[15] Ethically, God was difficult to live with, impossible to live without. Although an embarrassment to rational ethics, faith in a sovereign God was basic to religion, and, as Mahan put it, added "solemn and impressive interest to the idea of duty."[16]

The discussion of duties to God produced the same hazy sententiousness evident in other areas of practical morals. Wayland, for example, dealt at length with the duties of prayer, keeping the Sabbath, and cultivating a devout temper.[17] But through it all comes the message that the faithful performance of our duties to God is really the backbone of sound morality; that we owe it not only to ourselves and others, but to God as well, to perform all our duties, personal and interpersonal; that to love God is also to love our neighbor and ourselves, and to serve the best interests of all. Indeed, all our duties ultimately intertwine, as the *Encyclopaedia Americana* stated in 1849. Moral duties

> have been distinguished into three great classes—duties to God, to our fellow-men, and to ourselves—but, though they may be classified they are not to be separated. Duties to God comprise, essentially, all our obligations and when we serve other men, we, in effect, labor for ourselves; so, too, in improving ourselves we are qualifying ourselves to render the highest service to others.[18]

9

The Nature of True Virtue

The educated man of virtue, the product of the old-time college, was a man of dedication and integrity—a man who understood his duty and was resolved unflinchingly to perform it. In theory, at least, he was a man not only of good intentions but of good will. That is, he was not merely determined to do his duty in life, stolidly, impassively; he approached life itself in a spirit of benevolence and Christian love, and with a sincere devotion to the highest principles of justice. True virtue, in other words, involved more than acceptable or even admirable conduct. It included a concern for and the cultivation of good motives. This matter of motives was a troubling one for Victorian moralists in Britain as well as in America; and it is no accident that two of the characteristics most often associated with Victorianism, by the Victorians themselves as well as by later generations, are hypocrisy and earnestness—or that Stevenson's Dr. Jekyll, while admitting "a profound duplicity" in his life, nevertheless insists that each side of his character is "in dead earnest." The philanthropist may do a world of good. But it counts for little if his beneficence is a public façade that merely expresses private ambition or hides secret malevolence.

The question of motives, or the proper material conditions for the performance of duty, had been formally raised in the eighteenth century in reaction to the cynical interpretation of human conduct offered by the likes of Thomas Hobbes, who maintained that the virtuous person is motivated either by fear or by the desire to ingratiate himself with others. British writers like Francis Hutcheson and Joseph Butler criticized Hobbes, and those who adopted a similar point of view, for not giving sufficient attention to the truly disinterested emotions that move people.[1] But, although the frankly cynical interpretation of virtue was to suffer defeat in the eighteenth-century British debate, the selfish theory reappeared again and again in various revised forms. One such revision was that of William Paley, which was repudiated by the American academic moralists. Nevertheless, the moralist who is charged with the task of persuading people to behave well finds it difficult to abandon every appeal to self-interest as a moral incentive. There is, Mark Hopkins took pains to point out, "no antinomy" but rather a "harmony" between virtue and happiness.[2] Human nature being what it is, there is no harm in reminding people that good conduct is rewarding as well as commendable. Granting all this, however, it is still well for the moral philosopher to make it clear that virtue—true virtue—is not selfish or calculating; that the truly virtuous man, impelled only by a thirst for righteousness, will always go a step or two beyond the call of duty.

For the Christian moralist the problem of motivation is still more complex. The Christian is responsible not only for his actions and intentions but for his most secret desires. In the eyes of God, the hateful man is a murderer. In the Christian context, obligation is an infinitely expansible thing, and duty is thrust back into the deepest recesses of the soul. Morality is actually irrelevant. All that really matters is one's total consecration to Christ, from which all good follows. And those moralists who ultimately base their ethics on their Christian witness—whether they consider moral theory "independent" of revealed religion or not—are apt to find their moral systems freighted with a cargo of high explosives.[3] Christian ethics have always pushed toward perfectionism.

In Christian theology the idea of perfection, or perfect sanctification in this life, has been regarded with, at best, suspicious fascination. On the one hand, it is obvious that God's demands on man are absolute; and Christians have always found it difficult to explain away the command of Jesus, "Be ye therefore perfect, even as your Father in heaven is perfect." On the other hand, Christians have been equally moved by a profound sense of history and of man's existential bondage in sin. Consequently, thinkers of the Christian mainstream have, until the eighteenth century, treated perfection as a splendid but unrealizable ideal. Perfection was openly preached only among the sects or elaborated as an esoteric mystical doctrine.[4] It was John Wesley in the eighteenth century who, identifying perfection with perfect love, took Christian perfection from the realm of the recondite and the heterodox, and made it into a message for all men. Even Wesleyan perfection, however, was more a devotional ideal than a moral imperative.[5]

As a theological doctrine, Christian perfection, even in Wesleyan hands, was relatively harmless. Mixed into a moral theory, however, it could prove to be stronger medicine, and in discussing the nature of virtue American academic moralists found it hard to resist such a mixture. For example, in summing up our duties to others, most (but not all) of the academic moralists found it convenient to use love or benevolence as a handy rule of thumb, in accord with the Scriptural injunction to love God above all and our neighbor as ourselves (Matthew xxii: 37–40). Now to equate virtue with love, even loosely, is not an entirely satisfactory tactic in moral theory; not even when one makes it clear that one is referring to "rational love" rather than to some purely emotional feeling.[6] To be sure, Francis Hutcheson and other eighteenth-century British moralists had equated virtue and disinterested benevolence; but in America Jonathan Edwards and his followers had painstakingly demonstrated what a rare thing "true virtue"—totally unselfish and universal benevolence—really is. Virtue, thus defined by Edwards, became one with holiness, a condition possible only for regenerate man.[7] "Disinterested benevolence," the shorthand of eighteenth-century philosophers, eventually joined with Edwardsean soul-searching and Wesleyan romanticism to become purity of heart, the do-or-die imperative of the nineteenth-century evangelist. If one is to be truly virtuous,

79

said John Leadley Dagg, every action "must conform completely to the rule of right; and so must every desire." Even the conservative Francis Bowen insisted that the good man's motives must be free of every "stain of selfishness." Virtue that is not cultivated wholeheartedly and for its own sake "is not virtue but selfishness."[8] Christian perfection makes demands on our whole being, and is constantly erasing the morally neutral ground between virtue and vice.

Even those who both rejected the theological doctrine of perfect sanctification in this life (as most did) and resisted the temptation to identify virtue with benevolence, might use the language of perfection in moral exhortation. Such language may be found in the less cautious utterances of a James Walker or a Noah Porter as well as in the staunchly evangelical demand for perfect rectitude issued by Charles Grandison Finney. But it was at Oberlin College, in the thinking of Finney and Asa Mahan, that perfectionism took its most explicit form. Finney and Mahan elaborated their position in the 1840's, defending it from the lecture platform and in the pages of the *Oberlin Evangelist*, which began publication in 1839 and served as the lively official organ of the Oberlin community. Mahan, the president of the new college, may be credited with having given the first formulation of the Oberlin version of Christian perfection. He argued that the Scriptural admonition to be perfect implies

> a full and perfect discharge of our entire duty, of all existing obligation in respect to God and all other beings. It is perfect obedience to the moral law. . . . It implies the entire absence of all selfishness, and the perpetual presence and all-pervading influence of pure and perfect love.

For "Love is the fulfilling of the law," and "perfect love" is "perfection in holiness."[9]

Mahan was careful to distinguish his Christian perfection from what he called "perfectionism"—the antinomian "abrogation of all law" urged by John Humphrey Noyes.[10] For Mahan and his colleagues, the law—the moral law of God—was the absolute standard for Christian life. In fact, Mahan was so devoted to the concept of moral law that a leading Methodist spokesman, the Reverend George Peck, considered the Oberlin doctrine a form of "legal perfection," which departed from the "Wesleyan track" by "a confounding of the law and the gospel."[11]

Charles G. Finney's perfectionism was at least as demanding as Mahan's. Finney had begun by emphasizing the moral power of the divine truth upon the heart of the believer both in the conversion experience and throughout the life of faith. In 1841, however, Finney was influenced by William Cochran, an Oberlin alumnus (class of 1839), who delivered an address before the Society of Alumni on the "Simplicity of Moral Actions," arguing against the possibility of a divided heart in moral actions. Applying strict Kantian logic to the psychology of religious experience, Cochran reasoned "that the coexistence of sin and holiness, or of two opposite moral states, is impossible." Reconciliation with God means "the abandonment of all sin" in "entire conformity to God's law."[12] Cochran's metaphysical theory of the simplicity of moral actions seemed to fit the evangelical mood at Oberlin. After all, is not conversion an either-or experience?

Although Cochran's theory posed many problems for the theologian, since it put sanctification before justification and thus implicitly contradicted the basic Protestant-Pauline tradition,[13] Finney did not hesitate to introduce the theory in his account of Christian perfection. *"The Government of God,"* he said, *"accepts nothing as virtue but obedience to the moral law of God."*[14] This obedience must be "entire."[15] The moral law demands completely unselfish benevolence, amounting to a consecration of one's will to the highest well-being of God and his universe.[16] Nothing short of total consecration will suffice. Moral character, Finney insisted, *"is always wholly right or wholly wrong, and never partly right and partly wrong at the same time."*[17] Finney's evangelical moralism, with its relentless either-or demand, gave morals a new religious urgency just as it gave religion a new moral simplicity. Vice was no longer merely wicked intention, but sin. And virtue was now more than the resolution to struggle against temptation in the moral law: it was holiness or total consecration to Christ. Finney was at once risking an under-valuation of religious experience and putting a terrible burden on morals. Conversion, reduced to an ethical obligation, loses that quality of mystery and awfulness attending one's confrontation with the wholly Other. And virtue, confounded by what Rudolf Otto calls the *mysterium tremendum*, risks being driven to madness by the "overpoweringness" of divine energy.[18] The proposition "total consecration or else!" makes a grotesque summary of moral duty.

To be sure, Mahan and Finney took some of the sting out of their theories in their qualifications. Although the moral law is absolutely unyielding, for example, the law demands—may demand—nothing that is beyond human ability. Man's ability is as much a measure of the law as the law is a measure of right conduct.[19] Still, the law remains the law. And presented starkly in lectures and sermons—without some of the qualifying paragraphs and appendices of which Finney, especially, was so fond—the law appeared as a terrible all-or-nothing command. James Harris Fairchild, the successor of Mahan and Finney at Oberlin, expressed the moral absolutism of the Oberlin doctrine when he insisted that there is no distinction between the imperative and the meritorious:

> Works of supererogation are impossible to a moral being—the performance of more than duty. Obligation keeps pace with ability. . . . There can be no meritorious works that are not obligatory. No being, divine or human, can ever do more than duty, because he can never transcend ability.[20]

The law cannot require what is impossible. But everything that is possible falls within the jurisdiction of the law. God's moral law, said Mahan, applies to all the acts that a person "may, and consequently ought or ought not," perform in any situation. Scripture requires that we love God with *all* our powers.[21] To the perfectionist, the noblest human possibilities are not part of an ever-receding goal but an urgent command, to be obeyed here and now.

As a theological doctrine perfectionism remained unacceptable to most, so we must regard Oberlinite perfectionism as no more than a caricature of the point of view urged in the

ordinary textbooks on moral philosophy. Granting this, however, there are certain features in the Oberlin position—certain aspects of the perfectionist frame of mind—that shed
light on the wider moral instruction in the old-time college.
What we learn from the men at Oberlin is not that men can
be perfect or can render perfect obedience to the moral law,
but that they should strive mightily, stretching every moral
nerve and muscle, in the effort to do so. The features in
Oberlinite perfectionism that are of interest are three: a tendency toward moral inflationism, a mood of moral strenuosity, and a commitment to what may be called ethical pietism.

James Fairchild's contention that there is no distinction
between the imperative and the meritorious is an example of
moral inflationism. All the academic moralists were disposed
to using high-sounding rhetoric to express simple duties; but
few could be charged with taking the extreme position urged
by Fairchild. Nevertheless, the ideal product of all their
teaching and exhortation was what James Walker called the
man of "invincible moral purpose" who seeks out "the moral
aspects" of all matters.[22] The academic moralists, that is, encouraged the evangelical propensity to transpose all issues,
as one historian put it, to "the moralistic octave," thus ex-
tending the range of the moral imperative outward, into all
areas of life, if not upward, to the highest summit of human
aspiration.[23] It is in the psychology of Christian responsibility, however, that the tendency towards moral inflationism
is perhaps most evident. The Christian is responsible not only
for his actions, said Archibald Alexander, who was not atypical in this respect, but also for his "disposition" and "affections." The "moral governor of the World," he maintained,
requires above all "obedience of the heart."[24] Moral duty thus
expanded in three directions: upward, toward the highest
ideals; outward, into the world of everyday affairs; and inward, into the darkest corners of the heart.

The tendency toward moral inflationism fitted in well
with the mood of moral strenuosity. The writers of textbooks
on ethical science seem to have regarded the world as an
arena for moral athleticism, a place for the testing and per-
fecting of virtue. Seventeenth-century Puritanism had set a

precedent for this way of thinking, of course; and indeed the obsession with moral discipline and character-building was part of the Victorian temper.[25] The American academic moralists wrote in the spirit of their age when they insisted both on the cosmic urgency and on the day-to-day practicability of trying to lead what William Ellery Channing called "the perfect life."[26] Though a person may not expect actually to become perfect in this lifetime, man is nevertheless a creature capable of unlimited moral improvement. There "burns within him," said James Walker, "an instinctive desire for growth, of ceaseless progress."[27] An individual's moral progress was measured in terms of the refinement of his conscience—his ability to discern and accurately to judge the moral quality in events—and of the cultivation of his will, the habit of acting always in accord with one's sense of duty. All this sounds rather unremarkable until one pauses to consider how differently nineteenth-century and twentieth-century man view such things as conscience and will-power. Victorian people had a far greater trust in the conscious life and in the powers of will (whatever theological disabilities there might be) than modern man has. Since Freud's time, western man has found it possible to claim psychological exemption from a number of what had once been regarded as life's moral challenges. The man of virtue in the nineteenth century was expected not only to "control and subjugate" his passions, but also to be always alert to the moral significance of daily occurrences and to cultivate what was commonly described as a "sweet," "manly," and "benevolent" temper. If one uses his faculties as he ought, said Francis Wayland, "he will progressively improve; that is, become more and more capable of virtue."[28] Like other nineteenth-century moralists, the American academicians thought of character-building as a kind of extended military campaign in which constant drill made one fit for each battle, every small skirmish fitted into a massive battle plan, and even a minor victory over temptation contributed to a major triumph for virtue.

Ethical pietism, finally, lent to conscientiousness and will-training a tone of cosmic urgency. The study of ethics may be independent of theology, but moral philosophy as taught in the old-time college was no systematization of infidelity, as Jonathan Edwards once labeled it. Moral questions were to be approached in a spirit of devotion as well as duty. The law of right, for Mark Hopkins, was also the law of God. All our duties, said Francis Wayland, are "duties to God"; and our duty to love God, our primary duty, is the moral equivalent of gravity—the universal principle of attraction that maintains the balance and orderly movement of responsible beings in the remotest corners of the moral universe.[29] As moral inflationism made all issues appear to be moral issues and the strenuous mood made virtue a matter of sincere daily effort and exercise, so ethical pietism made all moral issues matters of ultimate concern and placed the gallant upward struggles of the man of virtue in a providential context. Regardless of how critical they might be of Oberlinite zeal, the academic moralists all taught what William James called "the ethics of infinite and mysterious obligation from on high," by which all moral ideals attain a "penetrating, shattering, tragically challenging note of appeal."[30]

The American moral perspective of the mid-nineteenth century, conventional and uninspired as it appears in its details, could have profound meaning in the private life of the person who took its assumptions seriously. It could make of such a person, if not a perfectionist zealot, a man of moral earnestness, self-conscious regard for his own character, and an ethical concern that opened outward into the wider realm of social life. And if one conscientiously turned one's attention to the social realm, the same habits of mind that could make for a morally arduous private life could have significant and unsettling social consequences. For, broadly considered, the ethical code taught at the old-time college contained within it a genuinely radical impetus.[31] To be sure, this radical impetus was implicit in the logic, the moral psychology, and the Christian rhetoric used to produce an educated class that was committed to the highest ideals. The intention, obviously, was not to produce radicals but to provide society with intelligent and virtuous leaders, and to see to it that the nation's intellectual class was not seduced by the "licentious and infidel speculations" that were, supposedly, so fashionable in Europe. The intention was to promote social stability while encouraging legitimate reform, not to encourage or justify radical social agitation. But the rationale for radicalism was nonetheless there. For the truly virtuous man was a man with an ultimate commitment—a commitment to a law above all human law, the moral law of God. And the virtuous man, in obedience to this law, was expected to see to it that his society could be counted a just and moral society.

Moral Government

10

The Moral Law

A major problem facing the academic moralists was the question of the authenticity and legitimacy of traditional moral values. Many thinkers feared that moral values, having been dislodged from their social and theological frame of reference, were losing their authority over the minds of men. In the final analysis, the problem concerned what Ralph Barton Perry calls "super-moral values," such as blessedness or divine majesty, which evoke attitudes of worship and reverence and serve as the final, absolute principle in matters of duty.[1] Once, Christian duty—"moral obligation"—had been affirmed through faith, not decided by the intellect. Behind rules of conduct had stood the eternal law of God. The academic moralists, as Christians, wanted to set forth God's law in their moral theories, but as moral philosophers they had to work independently of religious belief; and God's law, like any moral standard, had to be justified rationally, must not be merely arbitrary. In short, the American academicians sought a basis of moral authority that was at once religiously acceptable and rationally justifiable. The most suitable basis, which seemed to share alike the blessings of an ancient theological tradition and of the new philosophy, was the moral law, a handy counterpart of natural law and an acceptable translation of the law of God.

The idea of moral law, like that of natural law, was extremely protean and very useful.[2] Moral law was a supra-moral, ontological standard to which to refer speculative and controversial matters in moral theory. As a "law" it was both normative and descriptive. It might suggest a divinely prescribed set of rules (either revealed or rationally apprehended); a principle of order within man, or nature, or both; or a law of sequence and necessary connection, like that of cause and effect. The moral law was invoked at different times to serve all these functions. Francis Wayland, for example, at the beginning of his *Moral Science*, defined "moral law" in the third sense—as an "order of sequence," similar to Newton's third law of action and reaction. Moral law, thus, is "a form of expression denoting an order of sequence established between the moral quality of actions [right or wrong] and their results [reward or punishment]." Nevertheless, as he developed his argument, Wayland allowed the term "moral law" to include divine commands and the imperative structure of certain "moral relations," as well as the fixed connection between conduct and its sanctions.[3]

The value of this kind of ambiguity is obvious. To speak of the moral law as a law of necessary connection suggests a relation with science and scientific (natural) law. To speak of moral law as a set of fixed relations in the moral universe, harmonizing with man's moral nature, provides a basis for moral obligation—a built-in Ought in the nature of things. Finally, to speak of moral law as God's law places morality within the boundary of Christian piety; and if moral law is not arbitrarily willed by God, it is nonetheless God's law. When all three meanings are combined, scientific rationality, moral values, and Christian faith converge. What more could a pious moralist living in a scientific age demand?

The idea of moral law has roots going back into Judaic and Greek thought.[4] But we may best appreciate the academic moralists' theory of moral law by simply keeping in mind their classical antecedents, while concentrating on both their post-Newtonian fascination with universal law and, in particular, their Puritan-Calvinist background. John Calvin had discussed the "moral law" as presented in the Decalogue, but his concern had been theological rather than moral. For Calvin, the moral law, as it was presented to the potential convert, was like a number of damning charges read to a convicted criminal who is about to have his death-sentence commuted. He wanted sinners to confront God's moral law not as an ethical norm but as a "curse," leaving them no hope "but through faith alone."[5]

In eighteenth-century New England, Calvin's view of moral law was significantly modified. Joseph Bellamy, a student of Jonathan Edwards, insisted that moral good and evil are not arbitrarily decreed by God but are founded in the nature of things; Bellamy is credited with having offered the first coherent statement of the so-called governmental theory of atonement.[6] Sin is not a transgression against God personally, he maintained, but a violation of the order of things of which God is the just governor. Elaborating on this line of thought, Samuel Hopkins, Jonathan Edwards, Jr., Stephen West, and a host of others contributed to what amounted to a fundamental revision of the New England theology.[7] Of the New Englanders, perhaps the greatest champion of the notion of moral government was Nathaniel William Taylor, for whom it was a "favorite theme."[8] Taylor insisted that God is the "moral governor" of a universe guided by a "moral law" which prescribes for all "moral beings" a life dedicated to unselfish benevolence.[9] In 1844 Robert Baird observed:

> The great achievement of American theology is, that it has placed the doctrine of atonement for sin in the clearest light, by illustrations drawn from the nature of a moral government.[10]

This "great achievement of American theology" was not an unmixed blessing. If, in its "directness" and "simplicity," this moralized theology satisfied what Baird called a universal demand "for a Christianity that can be *preached*," replacing the delicate paradoxes of earlier Calvinist doctrine, it was nonetheless difficult to defend. A God who is primarily a moral governor is after all a diminished deity. The more earnestly theologians tried to preserve the divine glory —by distinguishing, for example, between God's arbitrary will and his essential (moral) nature—the more deeply they

91

became involved in the job of defining God, and hence in delimiting him. YHVH—I AM—once known only in his acts, was now known only in his *righteous* acts, the only acts permitted to him.

In developing their notion of the moral government of the universe, the academic moralists did not draw entirely on the New England theology. Moral philosophers were much influenced by Joseph Butler, whose influential *Analogy of Religion* (1736) offered a full discussion "Of the Moral Government of God." According to Butler, the fact that virtue is naturally rewarded and vice punished permits the inference that God is righteous and that the notion "of a moral scheme of government is not fictitious, but natural."[11] Butler's argument was theological, but, unlike the New England theologians, he used the idea of moral government as a tool of apologetic rather than doctrinal theology. He was interested in making the case for revealed religion, not in explaining the doctrine of atonement. Moreover, he was addressing deists rather than a fairly well-defined group of Calvinists. His argument, therefore, was more general than that of the New Englanders, and more useful to moral philosophers. He emphasized the fact that the natural world testifies to God's moral government, that, indeed, the

> natural and moral constitution and government of the world are so connected, as to make up together but one scheme; and it is highly probable that the first is formed and carried on merely in subserviency to the latter, as the vegetable world is for the animal, and organized bodies for minds.[12]

Butler linked the world of fact and the world of values together in the divine government of things. The natural and the moral governments "make up together but one scheme," a scheme which points beyond itself to the Kingdom of God.

American academic moralists drew on a rich tradition when they spoke of moral law and moral government. They had at their disposal not only the age-old idea of natural and moral law but also the Butlerian technique of analogy and the "great achievement of natural theology," the governmental theory of atonement. If the standard textbook argument went around in circles, it seemed all the more air-tight. Moral obligation—the argument went—is a natural fact that is evident in our consciousness and implies a moral universe. The universe is moral because it contains moral men and is engineered to serve a moral purpose. Man is moral because he is so created by God. God is moral because he has created and continues to sustain a moral universe. Witness, for example, the reasoning of Archibald Alexander:

> The feeling of moral obligation which accompanies every perception of right and wrong seems to imply that man is under law; for what is moral obligation but a moral law? And if we are under a law there must be a lawgiver, a moral governor, who has incorporated the elements of this law into our very constitution.

Thus we may demonstrate, Alexander argued, not only that God exists, but "that he is a moral Being, and exercises a moral government over us."[13] If further evidence for the moral government is demanded, one need only point out that by the "laws of nature, virtuous conduct is generally productive of pleasure and peace of mind; and immoral conduct is generally a source of misery."[14]

The idea of the moral law was especially dear to the men at the Oberlin Collegiate Institute, who were more under the spell of Nathaniel W. Taylor than of Butler. Finney began his *Systematic Theology* with a discussion of law, defining "Moral Law" as

> *a rule of action, founded in, and suited to, the nature and relations of moral beings, sustained by sanctions equal to the value of obedience, and the guilt of disobedience.*[15]

The moral law, Finney insisted, "is not a statute, an enactment." It does not originate "in the will of any being." Rather:

> It is the Law of *Nature*, the law which the nature or constitution of every moral agent imposes on himself. . . . In other words, it is the soul's idea or conception of that state of heart and course of life, which is exactly suited to its relations.[16]

The moral law, that is, is a law for men, designed with man's powers and limitations in mind. It is a law of right, furthermore, not of might; and the human soul bears witness that it is just.

Moral law implies a moral government and a moral governor. According to Finney, God, the moral governor, has the sole right to that office and is, in fact, obligated to serve in it: "His conscience must demand it." Surely he must know "that it would be wrong for Him to create a universe of moral beings, and then refuse or neglect to administer over them a Moral Government." By virtue of his position as moral governor, God has further duties, the primary one being to adhere to a strict interpretation of the constitution of things. "No legislation can be valid in heaven or earth—no enactments can impose obligation, except upon the condition, that such legislation is demanded by the highest good of the Governor and the Governed. Unnecessary legislation is invalid legislation," said Finney, sounding more like a South Carolina lawyer than a theologian. "Unnecessary government is tyranny."[17] The moral government, said Finney, is itself justified only because—in a curiously circular way—it contributes to the happiness of all beings. The moral government rests on "the nature and relations of moral beings," according to which "virtue, or holiness, is indispensable to happiness." But holiness cannot exist without moral law, for holiness is simply conformity to the moral law. Moral law, then, "is indispensable to the highest well being of the universe of Moral Agents, and therefore ought to, and must exist."[18]

Finney, in the tradition of N. W. Taylor, appealed both to experience and to the practical needs of the preacher in order to establish human freedom and responsibility and to crack open the block universe within which, to his mind, Calvinist theologians had encased the moral agent.[19] His theory of moral government, that is to say, arose from a theological or, more accurately, an evangelical concern; Finney was more interested in saving souls than he was in clarifying doctrines. What is noteworthy for our purposes is that, although Finney wrote on "systematic theology," not only were his real purposes practical and evangelical, but he explicitly treated theology "both as a Biblical and as a Psychological Question,"[20] and used throughout a rational and ethical line of reasoning. In his *Systematic Theology*, and particularly in the idea of moral law it presents, one sees the translation of doctrinal questions into ethical terms in the interest both of homiletic appeal and common sense. Like Taylor, Finney offered his theological statement not out of commitment to some explicit theological doctrine—such as the New Divinity or Wesleyan positions—but, as Whitney Cross suggests, because he rejected what seemed "illogical, obtuse, or erroneous."[21] Finney represents the moralizing of theology in mid-nineteenth-century America. And his treatment of the moral law makes clear and comprehensible the relation between man, as a moral agent, and God, his moral governor: God is no longer the remote and unpredictable Being he had once been. Whatever theological qualms one may have about Finney's moralistic and legalistic theology, one can at least see how this formula might well make God more real and even more alive to the matter-of-fact, practical minds of many nineteenth-century Americans.

Whether they agreed with Finney's idea of the moral law or not, the academic moralists generally turned to the moral law as the ultimate norm by which duty was established and God's righteous will was made manifest.[22] Perhaps none of these moralists had a greater love for the idea of moral law than did Francis Bowen. Bowen's interest in moral law and moral government extended beyond merely ethical concerns: moral government was central to his entire world-view. Deploring what he called "the division of labor" between the physical sciences and such disciplines as ethics and natural theology, Bowen insisted that these two fields of inquiry be recognized as inductive sciences, based on fact and systematic observation rather than on speculation and *a-priori* demonstration.[23] The physical sciences, on the other hand, should disclose the continuing efficacy of God's Providence in nature, and should reveal the ethical purpose that pervades the world of fact.

To establish the fact of God's continuing activity in the

natural world, Bowen argued that mind, and mind only, can act as an efficient cause. The "spirit alone moves," he said, "while matter is moved." And since God's is the only spirit capable of moving the entire physical universe, God's spirit must be ever active—guiding each trajectory, pushing the planets around in their orbits, giving each living cell its energy, directing each molecule of boiling water.[24] God, then, is "no longer banished from his creation"; nor is creation left to run on its own, like "a deserted child." The universe, he said,

> is not a great machine, that was wound up at the beginning, and has continued to run on ever since, without aid or direction from its artificer. . . . The universe is not lifeless or soulless. It is informed by God's spirit, pervaded by his power, moved by his wisdom, directed by his beneficence, controlled by his justice.

As a corollary, it is evident that the "harmony of the physical and moral laws is not mere fancy, nor a forced analogy; they are both expressions of the same will, manifestations of the same spirit."[25]

The material world is moved and directed by God. So is the world of mind, but in a different way. The human mind acts as an efficient cause, self-moving and free from external control. God's power over the human mind, therefore, must be indirect and based on man's voluntary obedience. This power is expressed through the conscience, which reveals the most commanding and authoritative law in the universe, the moral law. In fact, it is from the conscience, Bowen maintained, that we form the idea of law in the first place. In our effort to describe, for example, the regular movement and the immutable order of the planets, we find no metaphor more appropriate than that taken from "the stern monitor within the breast." The "awful sovereignty of conscience is thus extended, though by a figure of speech, over the material creation. . . ."[26] Thus the entire world-order, physical as well as spiritual, is a moral and personal one, governed immediately by an ever-present God. Bowen described a universe run by conscience.

In both Francis Bowen and Charles Finney, although in different ways, we get an indication of the significance of the concept of moral law for the American moral philosophers. It offered a cosmology—a moral cosmology—in which human values and human actions were given a new status in the universe, and the moral relation between man and God was clarified. Once the theological doctrine of creation had been sufficient to establish human responsibility and to account for the fundamental difference between good and evil. The concept of moral law offered academic moralists a version of this doctrine that had been brought up to date, a version more in accord with the Newtonian world-picture and the demands of the philosophy of the Enlightenment. It spoke directly to a need widely shared in the nineteenth century, a need for cosmic reassurance and re-enforcement that was expressed late in the century by the American philosopher, Josiah Royce:

> We want to know that, when we try to do right, we are not alone; that there is something outside of us that harmonizes with our own moral efforts by being itself in some way moral.[27]

The moral law, as read inwardly by the conscience of rational beings, was a constant reminder that, as Asa Mahan phrased it, we are "the sons and daughters, not merely of time, but of eternity," that our moral existence is part of a greater realm of being, one that both encompasses and transcends the human condition.[28]

11

Moral Government and Political Economy

Once it had been established that moral man inhabits a moral universe and is governed by a moral law, the problem of the relevance of moral values to the workaday world of facts could be effectively handled. The question was a nagging one for academic philosophers who hoped to train virtuous men for leadership in a commercial society. It turned out, fortunately, that the world of affairs was under God's moral government: the universe was so constituted that there was a pre-established harmony between virtue and happiness, vice and misery. This meant that the welfare and prosperity of both men and nations were a function as much of moral as of economic behavior.

The harmony between virtue and happiness did not, of course, make concern for one's personal happiness a proper *reason* for the performance of duty. This was a rather sensitive issue, since American social moralists from the time of Samuel Hopkins through that of Henry George and Edward Bellamy had made selfishness the moral basis of social iniquity; and the academic moralists of the mid-nineteenth century all resolutely opposed the reduction of morality to selfish expediency. Yet even Asa Mahan, who despised the selfish theory of morals more deeply—if that is possible—than any of his colleagues, was struck by the ambiguous meaning of *summum bonum*, which could be interpreted either as "virtue" or as "happiness." To Mahan it seemed that the "true solution is no doubt found in the union of these two ideas; or rather in that of moral fitness, or order." That state "in which virtue and vice meet their appropriate reward" is itself the supreme and ultimate good.[1] Such reasoning as this —whose foundation is the concept of moral government— allowed the academic moralists to steal the best argument of the selfish theory of morals, while preserving the integrity of their own theory.

The best available evidence of the connection between virtue and happiness, it was maintained, is man's moral nature. God designed man to delight in righteousness. Early in the nineteenth century Eliphalet Nott was fond of reminding graduating classes at Union College, where he was president, that "a life of virtue and happiness . . . exactly coincide. To practice one is to secure the other." For the "God of virtue formed every faculty of pleasure, and has made them all subservient to duty." God has so designed our faculties, Francis Wayland echoed in 1835, that man's greatest happiness "is to be obtained by conforming his whole conduct to the law of virtue, that is, to the will of God."[2] Most generally, it can be said that the happiness to which virtue conduces is the consciousness of exercising all one's powers (spiritual and moral as well as intellectual and physical) in the proper symmetry—that is, the consciousness of functioning according to one's true (moral) nature.[3] In a more narrow and worldly sense, happiness was usually associated with success. "One who pursues an honest and industrious course of life," said James McCosh in 1892, "will commonly be successful, by the arrangement of Him who hath appointed all things."[4] Considering the meaning of happiness in this more worldly sense, we get an idea of how the academic moralists were accommodating moral values to the secular interests of bourgeois society. The textbooks on moral philosophy were useful instruments in the secularization of traditional Christian ethics.[5]

One example will suffice to illustrate the relation between worldly happiness and virtue, as it was treated in the text-

100

books. Francis Wayland, in his text on political economy, dealt briefly with the economic and moral meaning of consumption. As was his custom, he elaborated on a truism: "Where the amount of gratification in two cases is equal," he advised, "it is wise to choose that which is least expensive," adding that the "reason for this is too obvious to need much illustration." Believing that some illustration was necessary, however, he pointed out to his students that a $100 gratification might be profitably replaced by an equally gratifying $10 gratification. His purpose was not only to save his students $90; he hoped to show that intellectual and especially moral pleasures are as enjoyable as sensual pleasures, and cheaper too. "The pleasures of benevolence, as far as pecuniary consumption is concerned, are less expensive than those of the senses."[6]

Whether $10 spent on charity brings as much pleasure as $100 spent on a good vintage of Chateau Lafite is, perhaps, a matter of personal taste and conscience, not to mention temperance scruples; but the saving is undeniable—unless, of course, one is inclined to spend one's entire wine budget on charity. In any case, the fatuity of Wayland's argument, with its mingling of moral admonitions and catchpenny clichés, should not obscure its wider significance. The academic moralists expounded an ethical theory that made too few concessions to the reality of social and economic life. Yet these men, exhorters as well as philosophers, wanted to reform the conduct and elevate the standards of men with day-to-day concerns and materialistic aspirations; so they tried to offer virtue the fringe benefits of happiness. They did this by treating virtue as one of the tools of happiness: the unselfish pursuit of right—and let the modifying adjective, "unselfish," be noted—is, according to the divine government of things, the most efficient means of happiness. Good intentions, made into a habit of mind, are not only the substance of true virtue but the key to personal success and social progress as well. Make righteousness your magnificent obsession, the textbook writers said in effect, and all good things will follow.

It is natural for the modern reader to interpret old-time

101

economic moralizing as part of the bourgeoisification of traditional values, observing in it the rise of what is usually called the Gospel of Success. Such an interpretation is not only natural but justifiable. Still, if we are to be faithful in presenting the thinking of the academic moralists, we must also look at their writing from the inside, as it were, and ask not only what they were in fact doing but also what they were trying to do. If we adopt this internal perspective, we are forced to approach the textbook writers on their own terms and to see that, to them, it was important that the economic realities of commercial society be reducible to ethical terms. They were concerned, that is, to prove not only that virtue pays but also that the economic order provides a key to understanding the moral universe. Their real aim was not to justify the ambitions of a rising capitalist society but to show that even such a society, with such ambitions, is part of the moral government, that traditional ethical principles are relevant to every economic order. To put the matter in somewhat different terms, those of the twentieth-century theologian Dietrich Bonhoeffer, these moralists were trying to "speak in a secular fashion of God."[7] As society becomes more secular, even the man of rectitude and piety—if he is to be heard and understood—must speak in the idiom of secularity.

This point of view offers a better position from which to understand and sympathize with the textbook discussion of moral government and its harmony of virtue and happiness. The concept helped establish the moral legitimacy of the commercial spirit; but it also made it possible to regard the economic order as part of God's design and as a clue to his Providence, precisely as nature and the human mind were customarily regarded. The economic arrangements of society, said Francis Bowen,

> manifest the contrivance, wisdom, and beneficence of the Deity, just as clearly as do the marvellous arrangements of the material universe, or the natural means provided for the enforcement of the moral law and the punishment of crime.[8]

Since the economic order manifested God's purpose, the

science of "political economy," or of national wealth, both inspired adoration and offered ethical instruction. The great lesson of political economy was reduced by Henry Vethake, president of Washington College in Virginia, to two fundamental principles. The first was the harmony of interests: all sectors of the economy are in ultimate harmony, and because of God's contrivance the pursuit of inter-meshing private interests is productive of the greatest good for all. The second was the necessary connection between a nation's religious-moral standards and its economic well-being: a nation's prosperity, in other words, depends on its virtue and piety.[9]

All the academic moralists accepted these two principles. The theory of the harmony of interests frequently provided the occasion for moral rhapsodizing. "All society," said Alonzo Potter of Union College, is "one closely-woven web of mutual dependence, in which every individual gains in strength and utility from its entwinement with the rest." Men, pursuing their various interests, "co-operate unknowingly, in conducting a system which . . . no human wisdom directed to that end could have conducted so well, the system by which this enormous population is fed from day to day."[10] Because of the divine arrangement of things, said Bowen, we are all unknowingly "cooperating with each other as busily and effectively as bees in a hive."[11] The wonderful functioning of the economy not only revealed God's moral management of human affairs, but also provided—for those who chose to look into it—an edifying example of co-operation and mutuality.

By revealing the necessary connection between national morality and national prosperity, political economy seemed to give the simple teachings of Jesus the status of scientific law. Writers on political economy, Wayland once stated in a sermon, "have incontrovertibly proved that the precepts of Jesus, in all their simplicity, point out the only rules of conduct, in obedience to which, either nations or individuals can become either rich or happy."[12] The connection between virtue and national wealth made it possible for American academic moralists, in the tradition of eighteenth-century

Scottish thought,[13] to argue that social as well as individual relations are reducible to basic moral principles. The principles of political economy, said Wayland,

> are so closely analogous to those of Moral Philosophy, that almost every question in one, may be argued on ground belonging to the other.[14]

Nations, like individuals, are under God's moral law.

The ambiguity of the word "moral," as it was used in the nineteenth century, was fruitfully exploited by the American textbook writers. A "moral science" might mean an inductive science, as well as an ethical science; and "moral influence" might mean a human or volitional, rather than a physical, influence, and have nothing to do with right and wrong. When Francis Bowen, therefore, essayed to discuss *"the general well-being of society, so far as this is affected by the moral causes regulating the production, distribution, and consumption of wealth,"*[15] he was using "moral" in contrast to "physical," and not in a sense necessarily relevant to ethical values. Nevertheless, when Bowen placed first on the list of the "moral causes" that are responsible for the rapid growth of national wealth the "character of the people," by which alone we can explain, for instance, the "decline and fall of the opulence and grandeur of Spain," the word "moral" begins to take on more familiar meaning.[16] To the American moral philosopher turned economist, it seemed obvious that a nation's ethical character has a direct and important bearing on its prosperity. On the "moral character" of a nation, Wayland observed, "depend the justice of its law, its respect for individual rights, security of property, individual and social virtue, together with the industry and frugality which are their invariable attendants." And, he continued, it "may not be amiss to add, that all true benevolence may be defended not less upon the principles of political economy, than of philosophy."[17]

The important feature in Wayland's discussion is not his observation that a nation of cheaters and liars cannot thrive, nor that a nation of altruists may prosper. It is, rather, his underlying conviction that the economy functions within the framework of a moral government, according to moral (ethical) laws.[18] The incompatibility of chronic fraud and economic buoyancy, from this point of view, is but an instance of a higher moral law, a version, in fact, of the old notion of sanctions. By reading obvious facts (fraud breeds mistrust and hinders business) as moral lessons (vice is punished), Wayland opened the way for the conclusion that the economy functions according to the moral laws of God; from which conclusion further facts may be translated into moral lessons. The economic order is an intriguing moral cryptogram in which ethical behavior is a technical factor in any economic formula, and the phenomena of the market are parables of the moral order of things. Political economy gave the old, time-worn doctrine of moral sanctions a contemporary relevance. Indeed, political economy served as religion's secular counterpart. John McVickar, who taught moral philosophy at Columbia, observed that political economy

> is to states what religion is to individuals, the "preacher of righteousness"—what religion reproves as wrong, Political Economy condemns as inexpedient—what religion condemns as contrary to duty and virtue, Political Economy proves to be equally opposed to peace, good order, and the permanent prosperity of the community.

Political economy is thus "the redeeming science of modern times." All the national virtues—freedom, peaceful intercourse, and "if possible universal peace"—are shown to be "the highest blessings as well as the greatest virtues," and are "supported by the all powerful considerations of self-interest."[19] Unlike the individual, society might enter the moral order by being bribed rather than convinced; but enter it must.

Material progress, even for a society, was not considered a proper end in itself. Wealth, said Bowen, "is a condition of progress,—a prerequisite of civilization." It is not in itself "ennobling" although it is a necessary condition for nobility.[20] The academic moralists regarded material progress both as a reward for spiritual progress and as its necessary condition. Part of a nation's material reward for virtue, that is, is to be treated as moral capital and invested in the cause of still higher virtue. As a nation grows, so does its capacity for doing good.

A nation's true progress was thought to have two distinctive features, each of which was related to the increase of virtue. On the one hand, especially for those moralists of a strong evangelical bent, "progress" had perfectionist and millennial implications. It was founded on personal piety, total consecration to Christ, and the striving for a new dispensation, the Kingdom of God. On the other hand, if we draw our conjectures mainly from what the academic moralists had to say about higher education, progress seems to imply the development of a national character according to European standards of culture and civility. It specifically meant an improvement in the quality of American life, cultural as well as moral, through the leadership of the country's educated class, men trained to respect tradition while judiciously responding to innovation and novelty.[21] Until around the middle of the nineteenth century, at least, progress involved both the fullness of time and what Francis Bacon called the "forward retention of custom." The future beckoned the pure in heart while it welcomed the refined and college-bred. In the later nineteenth century the pietistic and millennial element was considerably reduced—or rather modified into a combination of evangelical sentimentalism and what Henry May calls practical idealism.[22] Meanwhile, the more conservative cultural element blossomed into a concern with good character, refined taste, and civilized standards that supported the cultural and moral élitism associated with the genteel tradition.[23]

However a nation's true progress might be defined, the lesson of political economy as it was studied in the old-time college is clear. Both individual success and social prosperity were regulated by the moral government of the universe, a government in which virtue was not only its own reward but the necessary and appropriate cause of happiness as well. The moral man was again in harmony with the moral order; while the immoral man and the amoral society were informed that the moral order included them, too, and that it was decidedly to their advantage to conform to the true nature of things. The world of facts bore everyday witness to the world of values; and the realm of values provided the best key for deciphering the world of facts and explaining the mysteries of economic growth. A nation entertaining the stage of self-sustaining economic growth is a restlessly acquisitive nation. But, it turned out, the secularization of values that commonly attends such acquisitiveness really need pose no threat to the basic truths of morality and religion. For it was found that the same principles of natural religion and natural theology that manifest God's presence in post-Newtonian nature could, with minor adjustments, show his presence in commercial and capitalistic society as well. Political economy offered but one more way of demonstrating that the entire universe is testimony, in its every detail, to the sanctity of God's moral law and the efficacy of his moral government.

12

A Moral Society

In our examination of the idea of moral law we are confronted with men struggling to cope intellectually with a kind of cultural shock, the psychic dislocation attending the loss of old certainties in the face of rapid and bewildering change. As traditional regulatory institutions were modified or destroyed, a new basis of moral authority and certitude had to be established. It was necessary to find new ways to justify and sustain basic ethical values in an emerging capitalist economy. A similar situation existed in the area of political theory. Here the challenge to morality and to western man's moral identity came with the emergence of an entirely new kind of social order.

One of the problems facing moralists in the nineteenth century, not only in America but throughout the western world, was the steady social transformation from the organic community to the organized society. The community (or *Gemeinschaft*), associated with rural or village life, is distinguished by direct, person-to-person relations in an atmosphere of moral harmony. The society (*Gesellschaft*), associated with urban-industrial life, is characterized by impersonal, rationalized relations established through an intricate system of legal-political regulations. Born into the community, says Ferdinand Tönnies, one is "bound to it in weal and woe." One ventures into society as if into "a strange country";[1] and, in making the move, one finds moral relations significantly altered. For morality—traditional western morality—is personal. Jesus said "love thy neighbor," not "love mankind" or "love society." Morality is something that happens between persons; it is a quality of personal interaction. Society complicates and even threatens to negate this moral relation by absorbing it into an extremely complex system of anonymous exchanges in which personal control is lost and responsibility is diffused.

Consider, for example, what is said to have been the motto of David Crockett: "Be sure you're right, then go ahead."[2] The motto probably had a significance on the Tennessee frontier that has been lost in a more complex society. In modern society the "right" is seldom certain; and even when it seems certain it is frequently impossible, or even partly wrong, for the individual to pursue it. Both Thoreau and John Brown knew what was right. But both found it impossible to bring it about—impossible, even, to convince many who agreed with them about what was right that it was also right to "go ahead" and achieve it. In later years, William Dean Howells tried to establish the case for social brotherhood in his novel *A Hazard of New Fortunes* (1890); but he exhibited the extension of social guilt more convincingly than he defended the possibility of social morality. The old morality loses some of its meaning in the new society; and moral man loses his identity.

The textbooks on moral philosophy represent an effort to preserve traditional moral relations in modern society. In this respect, they reflect what Wilson Smith calls the "Whiggish morality" of their authors—"that middle-class civic propriety . . . that went into making a genteel tradition."[3] These writers believed that fundamental moral truths, with both traditional and transcendental sanction, could be forever preserved and would remain everlastingly relevant to the human condition; and that these truths were especially needed in the restless, practical-minded America of the mid-nineteenth century. Not abstract principles only, but a moral spirit or sensibility—a quality of life and experience such as may be found in an agrarian community—was to remain a vital part of American life.[4] The romanticism of such a dream was tempered, in the thinking of these men, by a classical regard for order and proportion in the body politic and by a dedication to the rational approach to all problems. To many it seemed that old-fashioned moral judgment and the ethos of communal life could be adapted to the conditions of rationalized social existence. To put the matter differently, the ethical texts were used as instruments for transferring village morality to the city; and they were written in the belief that society, like the rational man, has a moral identity.

If society is to be treated as a moral entity, the body politic must be considered more than a contractual arrangement among disparate individuals: civil society must be divinely instituted. In place of the historical model of a social contract, therefore, the academic moralists preferred the psychological model of man's moral nature. Man, that is, is constituted a social being, society being his natural environment. Mark Hopkins spoke of man's social nature as "a condition of his being rather than an object of specific desire." The evidence "that man was formed for society," in other words, lies not in a particular desire or preference for society but, more fundamentally, in a complex organization of a number of man's affections, desires, and propensities which cannot be satisfied outside civil society.[5]

John Locke had argued that God put man "under strong obligations of necessity, convenience, and inclination to drive him into society."[6] Men, "obliged" by their own physical and psychological needs and desires to live with other men, find it expedient to overcome the "inconveniences of the state of nature," in which everyone's interests are always on the verge of clashing with everyone else's, by entering into a social contract. Such, according to Locke, is the basis of civil society. Man "puts on the bonds of civil society" by "agreeing with other men to join and unite in a community for their comfortable, safe, and peaceable living one amongst the other." For Locke, civil society is highly expedient. But his utilitarian wording does not entirely conceal the theological dimension of his social thought: for Locke believed that civil society was ordained by God.[7]

The academic moralists of the mid-nineteenth century, interested more in public morality than in social theory, differed from Locke in at least two respects. In the first place, Locke distinguished between civil society, or basic political association, and government, the formal relation between ruler and ruled, the mechanism through which sovereignty is exercised. Although many American moralists made this distinction, they did not always bother to maintain it clearly, and frequently used "civil society" and "government" interchangeably. Their real concern was with the relation between civil society (meaning either political association or government or both) and society in the broad sense of people living together interdependently. With this in mind, we will not attempt in this discussion to distinguish between civil society and government. In the second place, the American writers were anxious to make the connection between God's ordinance and civil society (or government) more explicit than Locke had. They thus emphasized the argument that, as Mark Hopkins put it, since social beings must live in society, and government is "the great agent of society for the accomplishment of its ends," therefore government is, "like the family," a "divine institution."[8] Government, said James McCosh, "is of divine appointment being of arrangements made by God."[9] In keeping with their normative psychology, the academic moralists inferred from the social nature of man the divine basis of governmental institutions, making human government part of the moral government of the universe.

Some American philosophers rejected the social-contract theory of civil society altogether.[10] Many, like Joseph Haven, modified it in an effort to bring the body politic more tightly under the government of God. Man's social nature, said Haven, proves that government is divinely instituted; still, God allows man to decide for himself, through compacts, the form of any particular government.[11] However they made their case, however they defined such terms as "society," "civil society," and "government," these American writers were concerned to make social order and political authority more than a matter of voluntary agreement or convenience. The body politic needed deeper cosmic and moral roots than the non-organic, juristic social contract could accommodate.[12] Political obligation derives ultimately from moral obligation, they maintained; and our duty is not a matter of contractual agreement. Mark Hopkins, rejecting entirely the idea of government by consent of the governed (a result of his reading of the Civil War experience), wrote that the American republic must establish its authority on a "deeper basis" than that "of mere contract or consent."[13]

By insisting that political obligation is based on moral obligation, the academic moralists did more than underwrite the social order. They also put civil society itself, not just its members, under the moral law. Charles G. Finney, after showing that "human governments are a necessity of human nature" and part of God's moral government, concluded that nations, as well as individuals, are amenable to "the moral law as the only universal law." "Societies, as much as individuals," said Francis Wayland in a sermon, "are bound to yield obedience to the commands of God."[14] By placing human government within the context of divine government, these writers gave the former cosmic identity, and based political authority on what Paul Tillich calls the "unconditional" moral imperative.[15]

The textbooks on moral philosophy offered a remarkable theoretical expression of their authors' Whiggish social ethics. In them, moral authoritarianism and political republicanism were combined: although political society is ordained by God, they maintained, the particular form of any good government will depend on the "virtue and intelligence" of the people governed. Republican liberty and moral obedience were considered related; as Wayland put it, God "has rendered the blessing of freedom inseparable from the moral restraint of the individual."[16] The academic moralists knew that the old systems of social control, based on what Wayland called "the principle of fear," had to be replaced in the new republic by a new kind of persuasive moral leadership—a leadership which they, through their textbooks, would help provide. But their moral leadership was impaired in two ways. In the first place, their textbook prescriptions for good citizenship reflected a temperament that was politically fastidious and too prone to shun ambiguities and involvements for the sake of theoretical simplicity and moral propriety. In the second place, the textbooks concentrated too narrowly on individual morality, making social morality only private morality writ large. As a result, these theoretical discussions tended to be labored and tenuous rather than perspicuous and to the point; while it cannot be denied that the hortatory appeals they contained sometimes hit the mark, more frequently they were bland and platitudinous.

The political fastidiousness of the academic moralists is evident in the distaste they express in their texts for American party politics. The writers themselves certainly did not remain entirely aloof from politics. Francis Wayland and Asa Mahan, for example, were both active supporters of the Free Soil party in 1848, and both men, like many of their colleagues, were active in a number of reform activities.[17] But the texts portrayed the respectable citizen as being above "political strife" and what Mahan called "partyism," and as maintaining a moral perpendicularity that never stooped to political compromise. Philip Lindsley, president of Cumberland College in Nashville, expressed the common attitude in a baccalaureate sermon in 1831. Every American is "by birthright a politician," he declared; and it is his "*duty* to study politics." But one does not study politics by turning to "the narrow, selfish, local, party, personal politics of our village gazettes." Instead, one should study "the great principles of government, of legislation, of jurisprudence, of international comity, and natural and social rights, of political economy, in all their applications, general and particular, which are calculated to promote the greatest good of the whole body of the people."[18] Eager to raise the tone of American party politics, but unable to recognize the legitimacy of anything below "the great principles of government, of legislation, of jurisprudence," the academic moralists were in danger of substituting moral abdication for political responsibility by entirely dissociating political ethics from political life. They certainly provided an ethical rationale for the kind of high-minded social moralism, with all its strengths and weaknesses, that characterized the mugwump mentality later in the century.[19]

Not only were partisan politics treated as a distasteful aspect of political life, like sex play in a Victorian marriage, but politics in the widest sense were regarded with distrust. Francis Wayland, despite his own personal involvements, treated voluntary associations in general with suspicion. The pledges of allegiance one makes in joining most organizations seemed to him to undermine personal integrity and to dissipate individual responsibility through group action.[20] In some respects this position has great merit, and it is indeed heartening to find men engaged in organized benevolent activities who are able to perceive the moral perils inherent in even the most noble undertakings once they acquire the apparatus of a bureaucratic administration. Nevertheless, there lies behind this appreciation of the dangers of organization an air of aloofness and a fear of complicity that suggest that these moral philosophers, as teachers and moral mentors, were less concerned with probing the relation between moral ends and political means than they were with preserving the purity of the individual conscience. One who wants to live a holy and upright life, said Thomas C. Upham of Bowdoin College, "should stand aloof from the tactics of party, and whatever constitutes the machinery of party movement." The Christian citizen cannot assent to any means that "do not commend themselves to the spirit of perfect rectitude."[21]

We are thus led to a second shortcoming in the way the textbooks handle social morality—their too-narrow concentration on the individual. Wayland apparently believed that social morality is possible only if one unravels the complex web of relationships that constitutes society, and reduces moral life to a finite number of simple person-to-person exchanges.[22] The moral calculus of the American academic moralists had to begin with the basic integer, the moral man. The moral man, however, turned out to be an abstraction, a fictive being, who had even less social substance than did the economic man of political economy; and the deductions drawn from his postulated qualities were bound to have only limited application in the real social world in which people live and act. For example, the moral man may be expected to know what is right; and in a society of such men there is, theoretically, no possibility of fundamental disagreement except in cases of culpable stupidity or downright duplicity. This logic, when introduced into the social debate of major issues such as slavery, considerably reduced the possibility of a constructive public dialogue.[23] Indeed, when we introduce an issue like the slavery question into our treatment of the moral individual and the moral law, we see that our discussion has taken place apart from the real world. The textbooks in ethical philosophy presented a vacuum-jar morality. In theory everything would go smoothly if it were assumed that all things function according to certain definable principles. The moral government was, in fact, a hypothetical, frictionless universe. But morality, unlike kinematics, has to do with friction above all. Morality arises from the friction of human interaction, what William James liked to call the conflict of claims, the compromising of ideals. The public moralist who ignores this ignores too much. To focus too exclusively on the individual and his relation to the moral law is to risk precisely this sort of abstractionism.

The kind of difficulty such a position invites is exemplified in the way in which the ethical textbooks handled the question of the duty of the citizen living in an unjust society. What is the otherwise obedient citizen to do when government oversteps its legitimate authority, or (worse) when it orders him to assent to or to commit a wrong? There was general agreement that civil disobedience is, in some cases, justifiable, and that the overthrow of the government may at times be not only unavoidable but salutary. Joseph Haven, in his textbook, flatly states that civil disobedience and even revolution, in certain cases, are not only right but a duty:

> When either the public freedom or the public virtue, or both, are in danger from the arm that is appointed to protect them, then it becomes not only right, but the duty of the people to

resist the power that proves itself false . . . to its trust, and to effect a change of government.

In theory, then, civil disobedience and revolution are sometimes justifiable, perhaps imperative.[24]

The question that arises here has to do with the dual purpose that the ethical textbooks were intended to serve as far as social morality is concerned. They were expected to encourage good citizenship, thereby ensuring social order in America; and they were expected to promote public virtue by cultivating the public conscience of the nation's educated class. In the interest both of social order and of righteousness an appeal was made to a transcendent authority, the moral law, and both individuals and society were placed under that authority. As long as attention is focused on the moral man there is no difficulty, for the path of duty is reasonably clear and only one's duty is at issue. When, however, it is acknowledged that the moral man is also a citizen, there is the immanent possibility of a conflict of duties: the dictates of the higher law and the demand for social stability may not accord; clear conscience may prove incompatible with solid citizenship. The professor of ethics, in his discussion of political morality, did not satisfactorily treat this potential conflict between the demands of God's law and man's. The right of revolution cannot be gainsaid, Jasper Adams admitted; but would-be revolutionaries must make their decision "under the weight of the most solemn responsibility to God, their country, and mankind." He added, complainingly, "Is it not one of the characteristics of the present day to rush into revolutions with too little regard to the circumstances and consequences?"[25] The academic moralists, though able to give detailed descriptions of the more prosaic duties, understandably could not describe the limits of revolution, or specify the precise point at which loyal citizenship becomes complicity in social evil.

We may not, obviously, criticize the writers of these textbooks for not solving a problem that has baffled the most profound social theorists of the modern world. No intellectually responsible public moralist would have the temerity to offer a blueprint for revolution, attempting precisely to define its proper conditions and limits. Still, as writers committed to a "higher law" above all human laws, this group of academicians might have seen that something was amiss with their social ethic if they could make the destruction of government right, even a duty under certain conditions, and yet could do no more to define these circumstances than note the "solemnity" of their occurrence. What their social ethic lacked—what their entire moral outlook lacked—was a sense of cosmic modesty and an appreciation of the moral ambiguity of social life. Convinced of the reality of the moral law and of man's incontestable duty to obey it, these writers failed to realize that in times of real social crisis—times when the moral decision truly counts for something—it may be impossible to act in a way that is entirely right. At such times, that is, any individual choice of action or inaction is bound to be partly iniquitous. It may be said, for instance, that revolutionary violence is always evil; but sometimes it is simultaneously right.

Francis Wayland must have realized some of the theoretical shortcomings of his moral perspective when he wrote *The Limitations of Human Responsibility* in 1838. He recognized the possibility of moral uncertainty and error; and he realized that an institution like slavery might be wicked, while certain abolitionist tactics remain morally objectionable.[26] But he failed to consider the possibility that, with respect to important moral questions, there might be no single "right" course of action and that a person might have to make his moral choice among immoralities. To Wayland, it was inconceivable that we can be morally obliged to do what we ought not do.[27] Logically he had a good point; but the moral life is frequently illogical.

The limitations of Wayland's view of human responsibility are to be understood in the light of his, and his colleagues', central concern. Confronted with the moral doubts and frustrations attending the emergence of modern society, the academic moralists tried to devise a simple intellectual formula that would permit or restore a feeling of confidence in the eternal verities, and would provide a sound basis for

social morality. They wanted to promulgate a "public philosophy"—to use Walter Lippmann's phrase—"a body of
positive principles or precepts which a good citizen cannot
deny or ignore."[28] But in their effort to overcome their doubts
they overstated their certainties; and in their attempt to
cope with the complexities of social life they oversimplified
the moral life. Consequently, the academic moralists were
unable to do two things that would have enhanced their
standing as public philosophers: they were unable either to
inform public decision-making with intelligent theory or to
offer significant moral insight into the pathos of political
affairs.

Having said all this, we must grant that in the very limitations of these writers there lies a strength. In their distrust
of politics, the so-called "art of the possible," they helped
draw attention to the fact that the demands of social justice
may confront us with something that transcends the political realm and that forces us to reconsider our judgment of
what is possible. Looking through politics to the moral ideal,
these students of what was called the "science of what ought
to be" struggled to keep moral values and a moral sensibility alive in a nation that could, at times, be brutal and cal-
lous. In their economic moralism (or moralistic economics),
furthermore, in their feeling for the relation between economics and ethics, the material and the moral, these philosophers contributed to the tradition of nineteenth-century
progressive thinking so well described by Daniel Aaron—a
tradition that includes Henry George, Edward Bellamy,
Henry Demarest Lloyd, and William Dean Howells.[29] Finally, in their search for simplicity and certainty they helped
sustain confidence in the reality of a higher law. That is to
say, they caused their countrymen to admit to themselves
that the political arena does not define the limits of the right,
and that human laws and institutions are not the final court
of appeals in the quest for social justice.

These textbook writers, as we have seen, were not aware
that they were contributing to a style of thought that was
implicitly radical. Nor was their suspicion of the political
process always solidly grounded in empirical investigation.

Still, there is an element in social morality that goes beyond human reason and individual intentions; and a nation's moral consciousness may be said to grow—much as its law —in directions that those who shape and interpret it do not intend. It is in part due to the American academic moralists of the old-time college that the American people in the mid-nineteenth century were not allowed to forget that morality transcends politics and that, in William Henry Seward's words, "there is a higher law than the Constitution."[30]

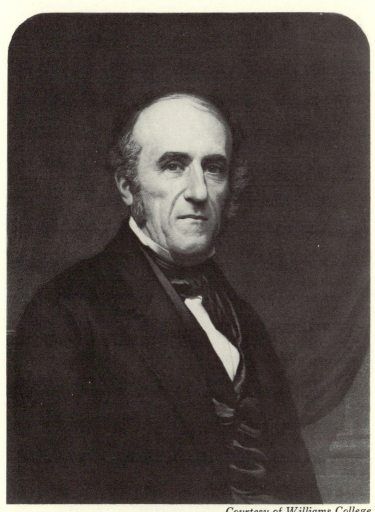

Mark Hopkins

James McCosh

Courtesy of the Brown University Archives

Francis Wayland

Francis Bowen

Asa Mahan

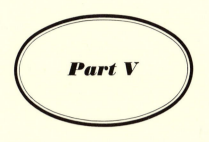

Part V

An American
Moral Perspective

13

The Passing of
Moral Philosophy

On the fifth of August, 1858, Francis Wayland partici-
pated in the celebration of the fiftieth anniversary of the
Andover Theological Seminary. In his address, Wayland,
like the other alumni who spoke, looked back to the old days
when the seminary stood as a mighty fortress of Puritan
orthodoxy against the onslaughts of all heresies, "antient or
modern." He recalled the time, back in 1816, when he had
first travelled from his home in Troy, New York, to Andover
as a prospective divinity student—a trip that had taken four
full days. On the last leg of his journey, leaving Boston, he
had discovered that he was sharing his coach with none
other than Moses Stuart, the respected Professor of Sacred
Literature at Andover. Wayland had listened in respectful
silence as Stuart and his companion, the Reverend Sereno
Dwight, staunch Calvinists both, discussed the Unitarian
controversy. Stuart, Wayland recalled, had spoken with
"unshaken, elastic, and joyous confidence," always ready,
like Job's war horse, to do battle for the Lord and for "the
triumph of truth." Wayland had barely finished reminiscing
when his audience was overcome with excitement at the sud-
den arrival of a newspaper, fresh from Boston, announcing
the successful completion of a trans-Atlantic telegraph cable
that very day. There were hearty cheers. Men waved their

123

hats and pounded on the tables, while some wept for joy. There was a cry for a prayer of thanksgiving, and the company broke into song—"Jesus shall reign where e'er the sun. . . ."[1]

The story blends retrospect and prospect interestingly. Even as Wayland was looking backwards to recall old heroes in past wars his world was moving briskly towards the millennium. The very faith that Andover had been established to defend—modified here and there, perhaps, to meet the changing demands of triumphant truth—was to be carried across the oceans by the wondrous application of scientific principles; and the triumph of truth would ultimately mean the reign of Christ over all the earth. The tide had been turned against those infidels who had tried to undermine faith by the misuse of science. Emerson Davis could confidently affirm, in 1851, that "we have no fears for the result; we believe that Science, as heretofore, will prove herself to be the handmaid of Religion."[2] And if technology, as Thoreau charged, offered only an improved means to an unimproved end, the reason was that the great end of Christianity could not and ought not to be "improved." The trans-Atlantic cable was carrying an old faith to the new world of the future. Francis Wayland and the enthusiastic alumni at Andover's golden anniversary knew that reverence for the truths of the past need not preclude belief in progress.

In spite of all the political and moral turmoil America was suffering in the 1850's, this kind of hopefulness was still possible and frequently expressed. In 1851 Mark Hopkins compared American society to a maturing person who, gaining increasing control over his previously undisciplined faculties, is ready at last to pursue his true end—the full development of his spiritual powers. Hopkins was optimistic about the past half-century which, he noted, had witnessed three important developments. The first was "the subjugation of the powers of nature to the use of men" through technology. The second was the extension "of the liberty and rights of the individual man" and the appearance of a new respect for the individual's private judgment. The third was the expansion of "benevolent and reformatory" movements, which had increasingly brought "human conduct and institutions into conformity with the idea of right." These developments, said Hopkins, especially the third, "are a natural, and almost necessary, preparation" for the eventual triumph of Christianity in society.[3]

The American academic moralists of the mid-nineteenth century could enjoy a measure of satisfaction, knowing that they were playing a part in this triumph. They had hoped, in the language of the time, to "impress" the old moral values on a new order of things, seeing to it that goodness kept pace with technology. They had labored to make the liberated judgment of the individual morally responsible. They had kept the "idea of right" always before the eyes of their countrymen. And they had demonstrated that the highest moral principles are really one with the goals of Christianity. Accepting material, intellectual, and social progress, these moral philosophers now looked for corresponding moral progress—that is, the progressive realization of old ideals.

In their dual commitment to the values of the past and the promise of the future, the academic moralists helped their countrymen through a difficult time of transition.[4] They helped propagate a myth of continuity that their generation sorely needed. And if, to some extent, they wrote their textbooks in intellectual isolation and were more concerned with inherited belief than they were with fresh insight,[5] still they made it seem that traditional Christian morals were rational, fundamentally unchanging, and universal. Consequently, the college-trained businessman, the attorney, the parish minister, the politician could feel secure that behind his moral perspective was the scholarship of a Mark Hopkins or a Francis Wayland—a man who had puzzled over the matter, and whose theories had to be right because they issued in such a sensible code of practical morals. The academic moralists were, to this extent, as Noah Porter had hoped they would be, the "navigators" of their country's moral life, instructing the educated class in the first principles of sound morality.[6]

It is hard to be more specific about the immediate influence of the academic moralists in their own day. There is the testimony of former students who extol men like Porter and Hopkins as great figures of their generation; but such testimony is always suspect, especially when it is offered in a memorial collection of fond reminiscences eulogizing the man in question. Wilson Smith, in his study of Northern moral philosophers, has described their influence, as public moralists and spokesmen for genteel reform, on social issues in the antebellum period.[7] And certainly, in providing academic and intellectual support for good causes, the influence of these men is noteworthy, if not profound. But it seems most likely that the professors who taught mental and moral philosophy were important mainly as personalities. Their tenure in office was sometimes long; and their figures loomed large in the small college or university of the middle nineteenth century. This was especially true of men like Hopkins, Wayland, and Porter, whose influence on society was mainly indirect. Inspired by the ideals they had been taught in their courses in moral philosophy, students went into the professions, into the pulpit, onto the lyceum stage, and into the schoolroom to make these ideals (if not always the philosophical theories behind them) known.[8]

Both these ideals and the philosophical and social forms they depended on were to suffer a series of defeats in the second half of the nineteenth century. Already in the 1850's expressions of hope for the future were inevitably mixed with expressions of concern and even despair over the present. The issue of slavery, particularly, became a source of increasing anguish to many.[9] And, slavery aside, by the 1850's American society was becoming more mature, sophisticated, and secular. Francis Wayland, especially, became more and more disturbed about the rise of such urbane vices as "slavery to public opinion" and excessive concern with "fashion" and "respectability." Preaching on the "Perils of Riches," for example, he not only condemned "the insatiate striving for more," as preachers commonly did, but he also criticized the self-made man who complacently allowed himself to become ensconced in his comfort and respectability.[10] Wayland complained about the life-style evi-

126

dent at the fashionable resorts, "where fashion scoffs at the prudery which shuns the appearance of evil."[11] Worst of all, although Americans exhibit "an outward respect for the visible forms of religion," still "the present is, if I mistake not, an unusually irreligious age." The new danger facing religion came not from outright infidelity, but from new sophistication. "Instead of transforming the world to Christ," he complained, "we seem to suppose that the same end may be attained by transforming Christ to the world." We must teach Christ "a more polished address" and "accustom him to look upon fashionable sin with allowance if not with approbation, before we can venture to introduce him into the selecter circles of intellectual, well-bred, and thoroughly respectable Christianity." The truly sincere Christian may become guilty of the greatest sin of the age—breach of decorum.[12] Thus, while Mark Hopkins was looking forward hopefully to the eventual triumph of Christianity in society, Wayland could complain, in 1854, that the "church of Christ is sinking into insignificance."[13]

A new sophistication was evident in scientific thinking as well as in social behavior. As early as the 1840's, for instance, James Walker pointed with some alarm to the increasing secularization of scientific thought. It is not, he said, that scientists are necessarily hostile to religion. The truth of the matter is more subtle and perhaps even more disturbing than this: in framing his scientific explanation, the scientist is forgetting to take God into account. The "religious references in the case have dropped out of the chain of his associations."[14] In 1858 Horace Bushnell warned of a "new infidelity," one that did not deny God but simply ignored him.[15] Science, increasingly accepted as the standard by which things are explained, could satisfactorily account for the operations of the physical world while simply overlooking such matters as God's superintending and intervening Providence. In more general terms, scientific thinking was being drained of all transcendental and spiritual meaning; and this process—a feature of what Auguste Comte once called the era of positivism, and one of the problems

127

that had concerned academic moral philosophers at the start—was now destined to present academic moralism with one of its worst defeats.

In 1859 Charles Darwin published his *Origin of Species*, thereby introducing a scientifically credible theory of random and purposeless change to a world in love with stability, cosmic regularity, and the pursuit of higher ends in life. More than this, Darwin's work enormously enhanced the prestige of the scientific method and, as C. S. Lewis suggests, at last made it possible for the scientific revolution of the seventeenth century to permeate western culture generally.[16] The cultural environment that emerged from the Darwinian revolution would no longer be congenial either to the metaphysical assumptions or to the ethical conclusions of the academic moralists. The philosopher who wanted to speak in a scientific way would no longer be able to speak casually about God's grand design in the natural and moral universe; nor could he complacently assume the stability and ontological independence of the moral law. John Bascom (1827–1911), for example, who had been a student both of Mark Hopkins and of Laurens P. Hickok, and who taught at Williams College and the University of Wisconsin, stated in his *Ethics, or Science of Duty* (1879) that

> as controlling circumstances are always changing, as social life is ever unfolding, the moral law never remains the same for any considerable period, and is hardly twice alike in its application. . . . An absolute and unchanging right in action is illusory.

Bascom argued that the moral law grows and progresses with civilization. His allegiance to the old metaphysics is evident in his insistence that the change in moral law is not directionless, but a progress and improvement (he did not say by what standard the improvement is to be measured). His awareness of the new demands being made on moralists by the application of the evolutional hypothesis is equally evident in his affirmation that the continuing change in the moral law is a result of man's changing apprehension of it —a change that is the result of historical circumstances and cultural evolution.[17]

In the late nineteenth century, the physiological laboratory offered a new experimental approach to psychology that discredited the old faculty psychology, prompted many to demand the separation of psychology and philosophy, and made introspection—a technique essential for men who referred their cherished beliefs to their conscious experience —increasingly suspect as a scientific method.[18] For many thinkers in the latter part of the century, Herbert Spencer's evolutional cosmology and naturalistic ethics seemed to provide a more factual, if not a more comforting, description of the universe and of man's duties in it than that offered by the academic philosophers.[19] For others, many of whom remained loyal to the basic moral and religious commitments of academic orthodoxy, some version of Hegelian idealism seemed far more attractive as a philosophical account of reality than anything Scottish realism or English empiricism could offer.[20] In any event, it became distressingly clear to thinkers after 1850 that the old synthesis of faith and fact— the synthesis of traditional Christian values and Enlightenment premises that the American academic moralists had struggled to maintain—had been discredited as an intellectual possibility.

In American society, as well as in its intellectual life, the times were changing. In the second half of the nineteenth century the growth of cities, the rise of corporate industrialism, and increasing ethnic diversity created a society that no longer supported many of the assumptions of the American academicians and could no longer be explained in the moral terms they liked to use. The rise of the city not only brought with it the increasing secularity and sophistication associated with metropolitan life; it also introduced a new kind of anonymity in which the conduct of the individual is no longer under the close supervision of his community and the old moral rules lose much of their force in the face of new temptations. Industrialism created a host of new problems, not the least of which was the way the modern corporation was able to separate social evil from traditional individual responsibility. Meanwhile, the arrival of new immigrants spelled the end of the kind of Anglo-Saxon Protestant culture that had produced and sustained confidence in the old moral values. The illusion of moral certainty was undermined, then, by social as well as intellectual change; while, at the same time, the old moral rules were losing their relevance in an altered economic and cultural setting.[21]

Perhaps the most dramatic social development in the destruction of the old order had to do with the changing character of American higher education. The tradition of what Laurence Veysey calls "discipline and piety" lingered on into the 1880's.[22] But the old régime had been failing even earlier. The old-time college and its president finally passed from the center of academic importance, and the age of the university was at hand, to open new prospects and to make the limited horizons surveyed in the moral-philosophy lectures and textbooks seem narrow indeed. The senior course in mental and moral philosophy was in fact a significant casualty in the decline of the old-time college. Mental science was split up into the study of epistemology and a number of psychological, anthropological, and educational disciplines. Moral philosophy, as it had been, disappeared; and all the courses in ethics, constitutional law, political science, and sociology that were to take over the government of its several provinces would not add up to a replacement for it.[23]

In 1892 the last of the American academic moralists published the last of the texts in the genre. James McCosh's *Our Moral Nature* was no more than a short essay (it was only 53 pages long), published after McCosh's retirement from Princeton. Intended to bring out the ethical implications of his massive volumes *Psychology* and *Metaphysics*, it is a miniature of the old textbooks. McCosh began with the empirically evident fact of obligation: we feel an undeniable sense of duty. He moved on quickly to conscience as a cognitive faculty with supreme authority under the moral law, which is the ultimate standard of morality. God is central, he pointed out, in the moral arrangement of things: God is the sanctioner of sound morals, a kind of overseer whose holiness and power guarantee the goodness and efficiency of the moral universe. Virtue includes both love and law, the two working in harmony. And the

130

summum bonum of morals, the "highest moral excellence," also produces "the purest happiness." McCosh concluded his book with a careful classification of our duties—to God, to others, to ourselves.

Darkness had long since fallen for the old-time academic moralists when McCosh's little book appeared. A year earlier, in 1891, William James spoke on "The Moral Philosopher and the Moral Life" before the Yale Philosophical Club. He said that the moral philosopher's job is to know which part of the ideal "must be butchered" in order to serve the greatest number of needs. There is always, he observed, "a *pinch* between the ideal and the actual which can only be got through by leaving part of the ideal behind." This is a "tragic situation," he concluded, and "no mere speculative conundrum."[24] James was addressing new men and looking ahead to a new century. In 1910, John Dewey and James H. Tufts, in their textbook *Ethics*, covered the length and breadth of the topic without so much as a single mention of any of the American academic moralists.

The mid-nineteenth-century textbook moralists had been aware that they lived in a new world—not a new nation only, but a new social and intellectual environment. Within this new world they wanted to preserve what they regarded as the essential moral values and spiritual truths of western man. The task was both a noble and an important one. Unfortunately, they never fully comprehended the dimensions of their new world. As teachers they tried to reduce their subject to a simple formula that proved inadequate in accounting for the complexities of moral life. As public moralists they gave insufficient attention to the difficulties involved in applying *a-priori* moral principles to society. Even as philosophers they often seem curiously out of their time and but dimly aware of the range and variety of the thinking of their own generation. In the final analysis, their textbook philosophy did not explain the moral life so much as offer nineteenth-century Americans a plausible and comfortable substitute for it.

14

Textbook Moralism and the Public Conscience

The textbooks on moral science, as Francis Wayland put it, were meant to be "simple, clear, and purely didactic," covering both theoretical and practical ethics. By providing a precise definition of terms and a methodical exposition of a few central ideas, they were intended to impose intellectual order in the area of ethical theory where once there had presumably been much speculative confusion. In the practical area, the texts were designed to gather together the basic rules of conduct and to suggest the most efficient means of cultivating one's moral character. Above all, they were meant to instruct the conscience of those who would one day become America's public and professional leaders. Like all instructional devices, the textbooks on moral philosophy did both less and more than their designers expected them to do. And, like any educational device, they reveal something of the assumptions and aspirations of the culture that produced them.

The textbooks were commonly used, as Wayland recommended in the preface to his *Elements of Moral Science*, as the basis of class recitations. The text itself, he suggested, should not be used in the classroom at all, but the basic principles and illustrations offered in the text were to be mastered by the student on his own time, and were then to be recited in class, the teacher calling on students one by one. As the class plodded its way through the text, there were frequent reviews of the material from the very beginning to ensure that the student thoroughly understood the system of ethics that was being presented to him. Often, the text and recitations were supplemented by formal lectures expanding, clarifying, or qualifying certain arguments offered in the reading. This would particularly be the case when the instructor was not himself the author of the text. When the course of study is completed, said Wayland, the class "will be able to pursue the whole thread of argument from the beginning to the end; and thus to retain a knowledge, not only of individual principles, but also of their relation to each other."[1]

In the *Memoir* of Wayland compiled by his sons, Silas Bailey, himself a professor of theology, recalled his experience as an undergraduate at Brown University in the early 1830's—at a time, incidentally, when Wayland had not yet published his own text. Bailey's lengthy description gives us some idea of how a typical class hour was passed. Wayland, said Bailey,

> had no tables, but sat with his manuscript for the lecture of the hour resting upon his knees. . . . The members of the class, in succession, recited the lecture of the preceding day. . . .
>
> This exercise concluded, there was a rustling all around the room; papers were adjusted, and preparation was made for writing. The president's manuscript was opened, and the well-known *a-hem* was the signal for all to be ready, and for the work of the hour to begin. He read slowly, and the class copied. . . . All were intent to catch the thought, at any rate, and the exact phraseology, if possible. The lecture was written in full by the students at their rooms. . . . These lectures seemed to us more wonderful than anything we had ever heard. They carried all the conviction of a demonstration.
>
> At intervals, not regular in their occurrence, yet sure to occur somewhere, he suspended his reading for a few minutes, and, waiting for a short time, until each member of the class could complete his notes and give his attention, he would

relate some incident or anecdote strikingly illustrating the last point made. In this department he was most happy. . . . These anecdotes were drawn from any source that offered the richest supply; from history, from romance, from poetry, from common, unrecorded, every-day life. Often they were mirthful, sometimes ludicrous. Frequently statistics came at his bidding, and always did capital service. . . . Hands and arms having been rested, the reading was resumed, and the lecture advanced to the stroke of the bell.

After the hour, concludes Bailey, the students would gather in twos and threes, making the lecture "the theme of the most earnest conversation." And the "mental machinery was still in motion when, on the following day, the class was again summoned to that unpretending room."[2]

However disagreeable this system of instruction may seem to the modern reader, it was part of an approach to higher education that apparently provided intellectual stimulation for some, and did not, as Harvard did for Henry Adams, merely leave "an autobiographical blank" for all students.[3] Wayland's course represents what Herbert W. Schneider has called a kind of philosophical "orthodoxy," a concern with systematic philosophical instruction—one might even say indoctrination—rather than with speculative or critical inquiry.[4] The textbooks on moral philosophy represented and gave systematic form to some of the central beliefs and ideals of mid-nineteenth-century American society. They depicted a moral universe that was orderly and comprehensible even to the ordinary layman. "It is pleasant to reflect that God hath arranged his providence and so constituted mankind," said James McCosh, "that it does not require an acquaintance with abstruse science to enable them to rise of a knowledge of God." "I suppose," Wayland once wrote,

> that everything that is to be taught may be resolved into certain elementary truths. These are usually simple, and if presented in a simple form, may be easily apprehended by persons of sufficient age and common understanding.[5]

If the demand for simplicity caused the authors of these texts, on occasion, to overlook or underestimate the complex-

135

ity of experience, it also permitted them to reach out beyond the walls of the college and to speak to and for a wider community. Their texts express, more accurately than any other body of writings, the "official metaphysic"[6] of mid-nineteenth-century America.

Before turning to the main tenets of this official intellectual code, it is well to consider what purposes it served by examining the social and intellectual context in which it was expounded. Between the 1830's and the 1870's, the period when the texts were written, the mood of the country was significantly altered: the nation moved from an era of popular excitement, intellectual exploration, and evangelical fervor to one of conservatism, organization, and greater secularity.[7] Interpreted in the context of these changing times, the textbooks on moral philosophy prove to be a curious mixture of the adventurous and the conservative, and their cultural significance becomes apparent.

The moral theories and maxims offered in the textbooks accomplished many things. They not only signalled an official academic rejection of Paleyan utilitarianism in a country which, many felt, needed no philosophical justification for practicality; but they also offered a coherent and formal philosophy that expressed the temper of American evangelical Protestantism.[8] They codified a general evangelical ethic to which middle-class Protestant America could assent, offering a degree of intellectual unity in a time of denominational and doctrinal diversity, and providing a measure of philosophical stability for a society that was, in the early nineteenth century, restless and often tumultuous. The nineteenth century witnesses an increasing secularity in American as in western culture, which these textbooks reflect both in the effort to offer moral theory independently of theological dogmatics and in the attempt to preserve the spirit of Christianity while acknowledging the demands of a changing intellectual climate. They reflect changing times while serving as a stabilizing and reassuring influence, adjusting, as Perry Miller said, "the conception of mind to a reality that was racing dizzily through the process of transformation."[9]

To put the matter differently, the textbooks on moral phi-

losophy form the intellectual core of the Victorian ethic in
America. In America as in Britain, Victorian moralism represents a secularization of religious devotion and piety. The
authority of the Church and of Scripture was being replaced
by that of the private conscience, as G. Stanley Hall noted;
and many sought an authentic secular analogue to the devout spirit. The Victorians wanted to restore a lost sense of
legitimate authority, to reawaken moral passions once kin-
dled by faith, to revitalize a diminishing capacity for ontological wonder without resorting to special revelation,
sectarian dogma, or arbitrary personal assertion. They
wanted a revised description of the universe and of man's
place in it that would once again give intellectual support to
what William Kingdon Clifford called "cosmic emotion"—
the feeling of awe in contemplating the universe and of reverence in examining our own inward nature.[10] Clifford, an
atheist, sought a scientific cosmology to replace the traditional one offered by Christian theology and sustained by
faith. In this respect he represents an extreme position not
taken by most Victorians, certainly not by most Americans.
Indeed, the American academic moralists wanted to preserve Christianity, not replace it: they used moral philosophy both as a secular supplement to and as an ethical
justification of religious faith. But the fact remains that morality, both theoretical and practical, offered the nineteenth
century that kind of common ground for affirmation and
conduct that had once been provided by religious doctrine
and practical piety. A re-enforced sense of duty compensated
psychologically for a waning sense of the divine. And, in
America, public ethics and civil religion replaced outgrown
and outworn dogmas as the basis for the nation's public
philosophy. This, paradoxically, was the result not only of
secularization but of an emerging pattern of denomination-
alism that was making anything less than the most general
religious appeal increasingly a delicate matter. In any
event, a kind of pious moralism came to satisfy both the
public and private demands that in this country had once
been met by traditional religion. Morality served at once as
"the common law of the land," in Francis Grund's words,

137

and as the basis for the inward discipline of the mind and the pursuit of the spiritually strenuous life. Starting with the private conscience, moral philosophy opened outward, revealing one's responsibilities to the human community and one's relationship with God.

We must not claim too much for the textbooks on moral philosophy, of course. Their stated purpose was limited and their immediate objectives were modest. Nevertheless, the authors of these works were concerned to establish a connection between secular morality and religious devotion; and their texts did in fact harness and transform the energies of American evangelicalism. In the process, the texts were themselves infused with evangelical sentiment, and the moral philosophy they presented was subtly altered. Virtue took on athletic qualities that transcended any Ciceronian definition, and the conscience became something more than what we usually think of as a sense of responsibility. As religion was moralized, morality was evangelized. In combining pietism and public moralism, the Victorian Americans, intending both to inspire the heart and to shape and instruct the public conscience, produced an official moral code that was more elaborately delineated and widely promulgated than anything produced across the Atlantic.[11]

What was this official moral code of mid-nineteenth-century America? At its center, as Walter Lippmann has observed in all moral codes, we find a picture of human nature, a map of the universe, and—if not a version of history—an image of society.[12] Let us bring together the themes that have been treated in detail in the preceding chapters in order to give some indication of the unified and comprehensive world-picture they provide.

I. *Man.* Man was regarded as pre-eminently a moral being, a creature, that is, possessing a moral nature and therefore capable of acting in ways worthy of praise or blame. Man's moral nature includes the ability rationally to distinguish right from wrong (good from evil), and to discover the path of moral duty. It also includes the ability to act in conformity with the moral judgment, doing what one knows to be right, eschewing what is wrong. To be sure, man is

138

conceived in sin, and since Adam's fall his heart is turned against God and his judgment is frequently corrupt. Nevertheless, given a proper upbringing and a well-structured education, man is basically trustworthy and can accept responsibility for himself. The matter to be emphasized is not man's sinfulness (although it is not to be lost sight of either) but man's rationality, his moral constitution, and the need to teach him to discipline and regulate all his powers, higher and lower, for the benefit of all. Above all, man exists on earth for a purpose. As a moral being he stands at the pinnacle of organic life, and the earth is both a moral training-ground and an eschatological stage on which is being enacted the great drama of redemption. Man is the key that unlocks the universe. His reason permits him to disclose the mysteries of nature; and his moral nature, inwardly examined, provides the best clue to the meaning and purpose of the universe in which he resides.

II. *The Universe.* The application of human reason and the scrutiny of man's moral constitution reveal a cosmos that functions as a well-regulated, integrated system, governed by both natural and moral law. The natural law, for example the law of universal gravitation, is a law of uniformity and necessity controlling the material universe and limiting the behavior of living creatures. The natural regularities represented by this law are to be discovered by the reason, because the natural order is a rational system that corresponds in its functioning to the operation of the mind. The moral law, though variously described, is in the final analysis a law of obligation, a prescriptive code with authority over man's volitions and intentions. Except for the fact that the moral law applies only to moral beings, it is in most respects analogous to the natural law: it is equally clear and equally susceptible of systematic study. Because of the moral arrangement of things, good behavior—behavior in conformity with the moral law—is rewarded while wicked behavior is punished; for, like most legal codes, the moral law both establishes an obligation and sets the penalty for its violation. One can, of course, speak of the moral law only indirectly, for it is not set forth comprehensively in any document, not even in Scripture (although Scripture is the best written documentation to be found). The moral law is a law of our being and is, as Emerson once said, the "open secret" of the universe.

The moral law exists in the context of a moral government of the universe, a moral order of things supervised by a just and benevolent deity, the moral governor. God does not arbitrarily legislate the moral law, for no being can do that. Rather, the moral law is an expression of his nature, which is perfect, and which is the standard of righteousness on which the moral law is based. (How God's moral perfection is to be gauged was never clearly established, and presents, in fact, an insoluble metaphysical puzzle.) It is God's person and his benevolent purpose with respect to his creatures that lend ontological status to the moral law; and, as the enforcement of any law is the pragmatic test of its existence, it is God who sees to it that the moral law is enforced, if not always in this world then in the next. With respect to this last matter, should further proof be required, the contrast between the peaceful expectation with which a good man faces death and the fearful apprehension that haunts the wicked man's final hours is a clear indication that virtue and vice will not go forever without receiving their just deserts.

III. *Society.* Societies, like men, live under the moral law and are expected to conform to its dictates. The lessons of political economy are essentially the teachings of Jesus applied to nations; what the individual is expected to do from a sense of decency, however, the nation is advised to do as a matter of expediency. Both the justness of a nation's internal and foreign policy and the moral character of its people are to be considered as factors in its prosperity. "Shew me a people who esteem highly the advantages of religion, of morals, and of education," Henry Vethake said, and "I will shew you a people among whom wages are high."[13] Moral motives are irrelevant in the functioning of the market-place, to be sure; but both the market and the men in it are regulated by moral as well as natural law. Although you cannot always explain a drop in the price of cotton in terms of virtue and vice, you can perceive a correlation between a nation's general well-being and its ethical character.

Of all societies, American society was considered unique. In past societies, said Francis Wayland in 1825, the "people were treated like a ferocious monster" that had to be forcibly restrained by coercive institutions. America is a free and open society, based not on force but on "the intellectual and moral character of every class of our citizens." As long "as our people remain virtuous and intelligent, our government will remain stable," and will effectively serve as an example to the world of the coincidence of liberty and prosperity, of democracy and order. The moral character of the Americans, on which this coincidence depends, is shaped by certain fundamental values that are indelibly etched in their hearts. "A Constitution written on paper is utterly worthless," Wayland affirmed, "unless it be also written in the hearts of a people."[14]

Such was the system of thought elaborated in the old-time college textbooks on moral philosophy. The system was intended to safeguard traditional moral and religious values against the assaults of modern thought, not only because these values were intrinsically worth preserving, but also because they were expected to serve as a basis for "a rational, moral self-determination," to quote Philip Schaff, which goes "hand in hand with law, order, and authority."[15] The theoretical apparatus offered nineteenth-century Americans the consolations of philosophy, while the moral rules it sustained provided the security of an established code of conduct. In spite of the limitations in both philosophical content and methods of teaching it, moreover, G. Stanley Hall, one of the most determined critics of nineteenth-century academic philosophy in America, regarded the course in moral philosophy as the "most vigorous and original" philosophy course offered in the old-time college, both in the energy with which it was taught and in the interest it was able to stimulate among students.[16]

Above all, the textbooks on moral philosophy provided an elaborate rationale for America's official allegiances. The pragmatists have sometimes been accused of rationalizing

American materialism and opportunism, the country's un-official ethic. The academic moralists of the mid-nineteenth century told their countrymen, if not what they wanted to hear about themselves, what they thought they ought to want to hear. "On the whole," wrote Stanley Hall, the average student

> completes his course in moral science with the conviction that there is a hard and fast line between certain definite acts and habits which are always and everywhere wrong, and others which are right; that above all motives, circumstances, insights, the absolute imperative of conscience must determine the content as well as the form of actions.[17]

This message, even though it expressed a moral absolutism that was at times hard to live with, and proposed high ideals that were easy to ignore in daily life, appealed to a nation seeking what Walt Whitman called "a religious and moral character beneath the political and productive and intellectual basis of the states."[18]

Nineteenth-century America's official philosophy was widely expounded through such expressions of popular culture as the famous McGuffey Readers, the Horatio Alger novels, and the well-known Boston Monday Lectures of the Reverend Joseph Cook; Emerson's hope, expressed in 1821, that ethical philosophy would be "everywhere disseminated" was thus fulfilled. And if this philosophy failed adequately to express the life of those who cherished it, if it contributed to the growing dichotomy in American life between what Van Wyck Brooks called "high ideals" and "catchpenny realities,"[19] it was nonetheless widely cherished and believed. A society in which the moral law, duty, conscience, and virtuous character are preached regularly is bound to be affected by the preaching. Although good intentions may not count for much, it *does* count when a nation believes that they do. The college course in moral philosophy helped the American people form an image of themselves and of the world—a moral image of life—whose tenacity permitted it to survive the evangelical enthusiasm that had inspired it and the philosophical system that had formalized it. Americans

were encouraged to suppose that complicated social problems could be solved by well-intentioned men, acting according to the highest principles, and clear-headedly reducing
complex issues to their simple moral components, thus making them matters of ethical judgment and responsible choice.

As their most lasting contribution to their country, the
writers of the textbooks on moral philosophy helped cultivate and justify what may be called an American moral
idiom, a characteristic style of moral expression that became
representative of nineteenth-century Protestant American
culture. At the basis of the American moral idiom was the
painstakingly acquired disposition to seek out the moral
quality in every event and to express this seemingly ubiqui-
tous element in terms of stark moral choices. If the style of
American moralism was of little use in meeting the challenges of the years after 1850, it can be maintained that
usefulness is no criterion of righteousness; and it is understandable that the American moral idiom would appear
prominently in the rhetoric of progressivism many years after
the academic moralists had passed from the scene. The
textbooks on moral philosophy provided an intellectual
foundation for such an idiom, making it seem that the moral
rhetoric with which the Americans scolded and indulged
themselves was not idiomatic at all, but literal, universal,
and truly descriptive of the human condition. Long after the
justification had been forgotten the moral idiom would remain—challenged, to be sure, but never relinquished.

The tragedy here is precisely the lack of tragic vision.
The textbooks on moral philosophy, like most textbooks,
reduced their subject to a systematic formula—a formula,
moreover, that was presented exhortatively, as much homily
as lesson. Since the subject treated was man's moral existence, this combination of preaching and schematization was
bound to produce serious distortion. For, as James Walker
realized, "simple and plain cases of duty are not met with in
life as often as they are in books. In life things are jumbled
together very unscientifically."[20] A person is forced to make
his moral way in the world of men and institutions, not in the
theoretical moral government of the universe; and not in-

143

frequently he finds it necessary to balance human decency against political expediency. In the abstract—or in a college textbook—the choice is easy. In practice, it is a person's most awful decision, ever reminding him of his own moral fini-tude. A person or a nation is often trapped among iniquitous choices, in a position from which there is no chance of com-ing through with clean hands. Here textbook moralism failed. It failed in that it neglected to teach the American people not only how to do what is right but also how to ac-cept the possibility that they may be wrong.

In noting the limitations of American moral philosophy, it is only fitting that we take account of intentions as well as results. For even though we are more tough-minded (pos-sibly more cold-hearted, too) than our Victorian ancestors, and considerably less confident about the nature of the moral universe, we are nonetheless capable of appreciating the con-cerns and hopes behind the philosophy they wrote—the mood of their thought as well as its form. Sometime in the 1820's, Francis Wayland wrote to his sister: "That is, after all, the most important part of a minister's duty—to live near God, and keep eternity always in view."[21] Considering Way-land as a moral philosopher, we need only add that all hu-man action, however designed for the time, takes place in the midst of eternity; and it is the most important duty of the Christian moralist to reveal the dimension of eternity in every aspect of man's moral life. Here perhaps is the deeper concern of Wayland and of the other textbook moralists. A month after his *Elements of Moral Science* was published, Wayland confided in his Journal:

> God has enabled me to prepare and publish my work on moral philosophy, a labor on which I had long been medi-tating. I have endeavored to make known the ways of God to man.[22]

Limited Wayland's moral insight was, and naive too. But his central ambition clearly was not limited. His goals were noble ones, and undeniably humane. In the last years of his life, during the Civil War, he was speculating about whether the Science of Duty could possibly be extended to cover the actions of men in combat. The academic moralists placed human conduct in a divine milieu, and saw in man not only what he is but what he might become. Their moral vision, with all its obvious limitations, was grandly hopeful. And, even when examined in retrospect, the irony of such hope can never entirely defeat it.

Appendix I

Biographical

Listed below are sixteen of the more representative writers on moral philosophy in the mid-nineteenth century—those whose published writings on moral philosophy set forth the general core of assumptions with which we have been concerned in this study. I have excluded several prominent figures, such as Francis Lieber and Laurens P. Hickok, who published texts on or relating to moral philosophy, but whose concerns and approach clearly differ from those of the ordinary textbook writers. Although I have occasionally referred to some writers not listed here, my study is primarily based on the writings of the following moral philosophers.

Jasper Adams (1793–1841) was graduated from Brown University in 1815 and, after receiving theological training at Andover, was ordained into the Episcopal ministry in 1820. Because of poor health, he found it necessary to live in the South, and accepted the position of president of Charleston College, South Carolina, which he held between 1824 and 1836. A good administrator, he succeeded in raising the standards of Charleston College after winning an initial battle with the trustees in 1826, when he resigned in protest against their restrictive policies. As president he was, *ex officio*, Elias Horry Professor of Moral and Political Philosophy at Charleston. His *Elements of Moral Philosophy* (1837) focused more on practical than on theoretical ethics, since Adams maintained that there is fundamental agreement among mankind on basic theoretical matters. He emphasized the fact that man possesses a moral constitution, and he gave special attention to the conscience, which he considered to be the supreme moral authority—that is, the most reliable means of understanding the dictates of God's moral law. Between 1838 and 1840 he taught geography, history, and ethics at West Point, thereafter returning to the South to spend the remaining year of his life.

Archibald Alexander (1772–1851) was born in Virginia and received his bachelor's degree at Princeton, serving as the first professor of its newly founded theological school from 1812. Alexander was an Old School Calvinist, and his theological preferences are clearly evident in his *Outlines of Moral Science*, published posthumously in 1852, which was based on weekly lectures delivered during the previous thirty years. Alexander is treated in more detail in Chapter 2.

Francis Bowen (1811–90) was born in Charlestown, Massachusetts, was graduated from Harvard in 1833, and studied in Europe for a year in 1839. Between 1854 and 1899 he was Alford Professor of Natural Religion, Moral Philosophy, and Civil Polity at Harvard. Though not a clergyman, Bowen found a major philosophical concern in the subject that provided the title of his Lowell Lectures (1848–49), "Application of Metaphysical and Ethical Science to the Evidences of Religion." His moral philosophy is considered in Chapter 2.

John Leadley Dagg (1794–1884) was born in Virginia; after only six or seven years of formal education, he became a Baptist minister in 1817. He served in parishes in Virginia and Philadelphia until a throat ailment forced him to retire from the preaching ministry in 1834. In 1843 he was appointed professor of theology at Mercer University, becoming its president the following year. From 1844 to 1856 he taught moral philosophy at Mercer, publishing his lectures as the *Elements of Moral Science* in 1859. This was a widely popular work in the mid-nineteenth century, perhaps because of its theological emphasis. Dagg is unique among the academic moralists in his insistence on the close relation between Christian religion and morality. He published his *Elements*, he says in his Preface, in order to correct certain deficiencies in Francis Wayland's popular text of the same title, which appeared in 1835, and which, Dagg felt, did not base moral obligation firmly enough on the will of God. Dagg insisted that moral distinctions (right and wrong) are based on the nature of God, while man's moral duty is based on God's will. Dagg's real contribution as a scholar was not in the field of moral philosophy but in theology. His *Manual of Theology*, published in 1857, was extremely popular and remained in print through the first quarter of the twentieth century.

James Harris Fairchild (1817–1902) was born in Stockbridge Massachusetts, and entered Oberlin College in its first freshman class in 1834. In 1841 he received a divinity degree from Oberlin, although he was never ordained. In 1858 he was appointed associate professor of moral philosophy at Oberlin, and also taught in the seminary. Between 1866 and 1889 he served as the president of Oberlin, succeeding Charles G. Finney. He retained his professorship throughout this period and for nine years after stepping down from the presidency. In 1869, Fairchild published his *Moral Philosophy; Or, the Science of Obligation*, in which he argued that our moral duty is determined by our assessment of the consequences of a proposed act for the general well-being of our neighbor. Nevertheless, Fairchild insisted, intentions, not merely results, determine the moral quality of an action and, consequently, the character of a moral agent. He thus opposed both narrow utilitarianism and what was usually called "rightarianism," an ethical point of view that considers duty as conformity to some formal rule or set of rules. "The good," said Fairchild, is "the foundation of the right." And the good is that which contributes to the highest well-being of God and his sentient universe.

Charles Grandison Finney (1792–1875), the great revivalist, was born in Litchfield county, Connecticut, but moved with his family to upstate New York when he was two. He was largely self-taught, and practiced law until he was converted, suddenly, at the age of twenty-nine. He worked out his own theology, which was nevertheless strongly influenced by the New Haven theology of Nathaniel William Taylor; in 1824 he was ordained a Presbyterian minister, although he was later to break his ties with the Presbyterians, moving over to the Congregationalists. Beginning in the mid-1820's, Finney conducted a number of revivals in the Middle and Eastern states; and his controversial manipulative revival techniques—his so-called "new measures"—won him both fame and notoriety. In 1835 he accepted an invitation to establish a theological department at the newly founded Oberlin Collegiate Institute; and fifteen years later, when Oberlin's first president, Asa Mahan, left, Finney took over his position both as president and as lecturer in moral philosophy. Finney's moral theory is clearly presented in his massive two-volume *Lectures on Systematic Theology* (1846, 1847), the bulk of which is devoted to the consideration of such ethical problems as moral government, duty, the nature of virtue. In the tradition of Samuel Hopkins, who elaborated on Jonathan Edwards's theory of virtue, Finney identified virtue (or "holiness") with disinterested benevolence, and vice (sin) with selfishness. Anything that falls short of totally disinterested benevolence is selfish, hence vicious. Finney expressed his qualified teleological theory in 1839: "I ought to love my neighbor," he affirmed at an Oberlin debate over ethical theories, "because his welfare is valuable."

Joseph Haven (1816–74) was born in Dennis, Massachusetts, and educated at Amherst and Andover, receiving his degree in divinity from the latter institution in 1839. He was ordained into the Congregational ministry, and served as a parish minister and as editor for the *Congregationalist* until 1850, when he was called to the chair of mental and moral philosophy at Amherst, which he occupied from 1850 to 1857. His textbook *Moral Philosophy: Including Theoretical and Practical Ethics* (1859), which was derived from his lectures at Amherst, proposes a "rightarian" view of ethics, making "right" the only basis of moral obligation and arguing, in effect, for the principle of duty for duty's sake: "We *ought* because it is *right*." In 1858 Haven became professor of systematic theology at the Chicago Theological Seminary; and in 1873 he was made acting professor of mental and moral philosophy at the University of Chicago, a position which he held until his death the following year. Haven distinguished himself not as a scholar or philosopher but mainly as an excellent teacher and as a proponent of a religious position that was at once liberal and warmly evangelical.

Mark Hopkins (1802–87), who is dealt with in some detail in Chapter 2, was mainly known as a great teacher and college administrator. He taught at Williams College for more than half a century, from 1830 through 1887, serving as president for much of that time. His two books on moral philosophy, published in 1862 and 1869, were widely used in the American colleges in the late nineteenth century, and were particularly appealing because in them Hopkins preached a general Gospel of Love that was his own blend of the philosophical and the evangelical. His greatness lies not in his scholarship but in his ability to communicate with students: his teaching inspired James A. Garfield, who was graduated from Williams in 1856, to define good education as a log with a student on one end and Hopkins on the other. He was indeed the exemplar of the old-time college president.

Philip Lindsley (1786–1855) never wrote a textbook on moral philosophy, but his baccalaureate addresses, delivered at the University of Nashville (Cumberland College) in the second quarter of the nineteenth century and gathered together in his published *Works* (1866), frequently deal with ethical questions, and reveal an aspect of academic moralism that deserves some attention. The baccalaureate sermon, in fact, may be regarded as the final lecture in the senior course on moral philosophy. Lindsley's sermons, like most such sermons of the time, treat the significance of higher education in a republic, and deal with such topics as the life of virtue, the true meaning of success, and the evils of intemperance, infidelity, duelling, and gambling. Lindsley was born in New Jersey and attended the College of New Jersey (later Princeton), studying under Samuel Stanhope Smith.

151

He was ordained a Presbyterian minister in 1817. After a few years in the parish ministry and a year as acting president of Princeton, he served as president of Cumberland College from 1825 to 1850. He was important mainly as a founder of colleges in the old Southwest, and has rightly been described as an "educational missionary."

James McCosh (1811–94) was born in Scotland and attended the Universities of Glasgow and of Edinburgh. He was ordained in the Church of Scotland in 1835, and from 1839 to 1851 served as minister in Brechin, where in 1843 he helped organize the Free Church of Scotland. In 1850 he published his *Method of the Divine Government Physical and Moral*, which ran to many editions and attracted attention in Great Britain and in the United States. This book was an attempt to establish the moral nature of God by empirically demonstrating the relation between "the providence of God" and man's moral constitution. McCosh's study was responsible for his appointment as professor of logic and metaphysics at the University of Belfast (1852–68), and his being invited, in 1868, to serve as president of Princeton, a post that he held for twenty years, retaining the chair of philosophy until his death. McCosh was a prodigious scholar, best known today for his massive study *The Scottish Philosophy* (1875), but known in his own time for his works on ethics, philosophy, and particularly psychology. One of McCosh's great ambitions was to formulate an American version of Scottish Realism, a lost cause in the late nineteenth century, but one for which he nonetheless fought gallantly.

Asa Mahan (1799–1889) was raised in the frontier region of western New York. He attended Hamilton College and Andover Seminary, and was ordained in the Congregational ministry in 1829. After serving a few years in a parish and as a trustee at Lane Seminary in Cincinnati (he was the only trustee to support the famous Lane Rebels after their anti-slavery teach-in), he became the first president of Oberlin College, a position which he held from the mid-1830's until 1850. He later taught at Adrian College in Michigan, serving as president from 1860 to 1871. Throughout these years Mahan taught moral philosophy, publishing his lec-

152

tures as an *Abstract of a Course of Lectures on Mental and Moral Philosophy* (1840) and *The Science of Moral Philosophy* (1848). Mahan was more widely read in philosophy than were most of his counterparts at other colleges, and was particularly influenced by Victor Cousin and Kant, both of whom he cites frequently. He argued that fundamental moral ideas are simple and indefinable—original and spontaneous products of the mind—and he was a determined critic of utilitarianism. Mahan took special pains to refute Finney's teleological system of ethics, which, he believed, led in the direction of utilitarianism even though Finney himself denied that his theory was utilitarian. (There was, in fact, considerable friction between the great revivalist and Mahan; and their quarrel was not merely philosophical.) Mahan was well known as a spokesman for evangelical religion and as a defender of human ability against the Edwardsean doctrine of man's moral bondage in sin. He was also the prime mover of Oberlinite reformism, active in every cause from the abolition of slavery to the removal of tea and coffee from the family larder. Clearly the most radical of the academic moralists, Mahan was something of a moral absolutist and a most difficult man to get along with. He once criticized a fellow temperance reformer who, against his better principles, was about to sip a cup of coffee. "Friend," he chided with characteristic humorlessness, "I should as soon, with that conviction resting upon my mind, take arsenic, as to do what you propose to do."

Andrew Preston Peabody (1811–93) was born in Beverly, Massachusetts, and was able to pass the Harvard entrance requirements with distinction at the age of twelve, receiving his bachelor's degree at fifteen. After attending Harvard Divinity School, he was ordained a Unitarian minister in 1833 and served as minister of the South Parish Unitarian Church in Portsmouth, New Hampshire, for the next quarter century. In 1860 he succeeded Frederic D. Huntington as Plummer Professor of Christian Morals at Harvard. He made few scholarly contributions, and his teaching of ethics was uninspired. Nevertheless, he was perhaps the most beloved Harvard professor of his time. Peabody was conservative in temperament, a trait that is evident in his two major works on moral philosophy, *A Manual of Moral Philosophy* (1873) and his lectures on *Christian Morals* (1887). He reduced morality to three "fundamental principles"—purity, growth, and love—which he considered to be self-evident axioms that were "intuitively" apprehended and beyond empirical justification.

Noah Porter (1811–92), born in Connecticut, the son of a Congregationalist preacher, studied for the ministry at the Yale Divinity School under Nathaniel William Taylor, whose daughter, Mary, he wed in 1838. That year he was ordained, and for ten years served Congregationalist parishes in New England. In 1846 he became professor of moral philosophy and metaphysics at Yale, and from 1871 to 1886 he served as Yale's president. Porter distinguished himself as a scholar, his most noteworthy work being concerned with psychology; his study *Human Intellect* (1868) is of particular note. Because of his wide reading and interest in continental philosophy, Porter's intellectual concerns extended far beyond those of the average ethical textbook writer. Nevertheless, his *Elements of Moral Science, Theoretical and Practical* (1884), derived from his college lectures on the subject, is not original; indeed, it falls within the pattern of works we are considering. Like the other textbook writers, Porter argued that man is constituted a moral being; that moral relations (like right and wrong) are "discerned" by the intellect, but not by conscience as a separate or independent faculty of mind; and that the norm or standard in morality is the "moral law," which is an immutable part of man's moral nature. In his ethical theory, he was described by a contemporary as a "rational eudemonist," in the tradition of Aristotle; and it is indeed true that, in spite of his emphasis on moral relations and the moral law, Porter's scheme was fundamentally teleological, deriving the "ought" of duty from the "is" of human nature, emphasizing certain "ends" toward which the moral man ought to strive, and depicting the moral agent as a self-regulating and inner-directed individual who is a law unto himself.

William Andrew Smith (1802–70), a Methodist clergyman born in Virginia, is something of a unique case. He gave up his career as a parish minister to become president of Randolph-Macon College in 1846, and showed himself to be as able an administrator as he was popular a preacher. In his course in moral philosophy, which he taught from 1846 to 1866, he used Francis Wayland's *Elements of Moral Science*, but he supplemented this with a series of thirteen *Lectures on the Philosophy and Practice of Slavery*, published in 1856, which constituted an extensive defense of the peculiar institution. Wayland had devoted about a dozen pages to the matter of slavery in the early editions of his *Elements*, condemning it but in a moderate way. It is noteworthy that Smith felt called upon to devote more than 300 pages to a refutation of Wayland's views. In his actual moral theory Smith again departed from Wayland. Although Smith spoke of the "right" and of the significance of moral "relations," he related the right to what he called the "ESSENTIAL GOOD," which was "an ultimate *genus*"—much wider in meaning than "the RIGHT"—that included "all *physical* as well as *moral* good." Smith's moral theory, in other words, was teleological. It is indeed likely that he preferred the more flexible teleological ethical position to the formal "rightarian" outlook precisely because the former permitted him a somewhat wider logical scope in which to make a case for slavery. Certainly his fourth lecture, in which he discusses "right," "rights," and the "good," suggests that this was the case. A moral philosopher who is trying to justify an institution such as human slavery might well be expected to be suspicious of the idea of the Right, which suggests an absolute imperative existing independently of non-moral considerations, social necessities, and extenuating circumstances.

James Walker (1794–1874), a Unitarian clergyman, came from an old New England family and, after receiving his bachelor's degree from Harvard in 1814, studied under Henry Ware at the new Harvard Divinity School. He was an organizer of the American Unitarian Association in 1825 and an editor (1831–39) of the *Christian Examiner*, the official organ of New England Unitarianism. From 1839 through 1853 he served as Alford Professor of Natural Religion, Moral Philosophy, and Civil Polity at Harvard, and from 1853 through 1860 as president of Harvard. As a thinker, Walker was unoriginal, and he became increasingly conservative as the years passed. He edited Dugald Stewart's *Philosophy of the Active Moral Powers* (1849) and Thomas Reid's *Essays on the Intellectual Powers of Man* (1850), making these rather ponderous works more available for classroom use. His own position, much influenced by the Scottish Realists, is presented in his two collections of sermons (published in 1861 and 1876), preached at the Harvard College Chapel. His discussion of the conscience is of particular interest. Although Walker, like the other academic moralists, insisted that man's capacity to distinguish right and wrong is rational and not merely, as thinkers like Francis Hutcheson and David Hume had supposed, a product of the feelings, he put more emphasis than any of the other textbook writers on the emotions as the necessary spring of action and the basis of proper moral attitudes. Ethical theory aside, it was clearly to the warmly affective virtuous life that Walker was most attached.

Francis Wayland (1796–1865), a Baptist minister and for more than twenty-five years president of Brown University, is a central figure in our study; his *Elements of Moral Science* (1835) opened a new era in the writing of moral philosophy textbooks in the United States. Wayland's text was extremely successful, was abridged for use in the secondary schools, and was even translated (into Hawaiian, for example) for use by foreign missionaries. Joseph Blau, in his introduction to a recent edition of the *Elements* (1963), observes that "early as he was in the American textbook field, Wayland had already grasped, in essence, the principle of blandness by which it is still dominated." Despite its blandness, Wayland's text exhibits concerns that are deeper and broader than the merely pedagogical, concerns that are evident in all the old-time ethical textbooks. Wayland's career and philosophical position are treated in detail in Chapter 2.

Appendix II

Varieties of Ethical Theory

When William Paley defined moral philosophy as that study which "teaches men their duty, and the reasons of it," he was, in his last four words, expressing a modern concern in ethics: "Why ought a rational being regard any action as his duty?" If one assumes that, by definition, one has the duty to do what is right and to shun what is wrong, the question then becomes, "By what means are right and wrong distinguished?" These are questions that most of the American textbook writers dealt with as part of their "theoretical ethics," sometimes with a surprising sophistication, as Edward H. Madden has shown in his detailed discussion of Wayland, Mahan, and Fairchild (*Civil Disobedience and Moral Law*, 1968). Since the eighteenth century these two questions—that of obligation and that of moral distinctions—have in general received two kinds of treatment, labeled by C. D. Broad *teleological* and *deontological* (*Five Types of Ethical Theory*, 1930). According to the teleological theories, a certain action or policy is right and, *prima facie*, obligatory if it promotes or may be expected to promote some end that is intrinsically good. Utilitarian ethics, which make human happiness the proper end of moral action, are teleological. According to the deontological theory of ethics, the rightness (and obligation) of an action or policy cannot be established by weighing possible consequences; right is a simple idea that is intuitively apprehended and is not to be translated into other, non-moral, terms. The fact that an action contributes to one's private happiness or to the general welfare, for example, does not entail that it is a right action.

There are varieties of both the teleological and the deontological positions. A teleological theory, for instance, may be egoistic, proposing, in the manner of Hobbes, one's personal happiness as the highest good; or it may be universalistic, calling for the greatest good for the greatest number, as Jeremy Bentham put it. A deontological theory, on the other hand, may focus on one or several abstract rules, holding that these are the general principles with reference to which one should always act. (One thinks of Kant's practical imperative: "Act in such a way that you always treat humanity . . . never simply as a means, but always at the same time as an end.") Or a deontological theory may hold that all judgments of obligation pertain to particular cases without any reference to general rules: a person merely sees that a certain course of action is right under the circumstances, and he formulates general rules and maxims as he reflects on how various kinds of circumstances may be classified.

The American academicians we are considering all rejected the egoistic teleological theory; and they rejected, as well, any version of the teleological theory, egoistic or not, that was hedonistic or that failed to consider man as a spiritual as well as a physical being. All rejected "utilitarianism." Significantly, even those who held theories that may be called "utilitarian" never applied that label to them. The utilitarian position as formulated by Bentham and the two Mills suggested materialism, worldliness, and a too-narrow concern with expediency. Furthermore, many utilitarians relied on a theory of mind that American academicians considered objectionable: the associationist theory, which reduced moral behavior ultimately to the pleasure-pain principle, and which seemed to treat man more as an intricate machine than as a child of God possessed of divine reason and an immortal soul. An American philosopher who did champion the utilitarian position was Richard Hildreth, whose *Theory of Morals* appeared in 1844. But Hildreth was too irreverent and his philosophy was too secular to be acceptable to the moralists we are discussing.

Those academic moralists who articulated a teleological theory of ethics frequently drew their inspiration from the doctrine of disinterested and universal benevolence—the unselfish willing of the highest good of God and the universe—associated with the followers of Jonathan Edwards. Mark Hopkins, for example, argued that man is a moral and spiritual, as well as a physical and intellectual, being; and that man's highest "enjoyment, satisfaction, or blessedness" is the result of his exercising his highest powers, the moral and religious. One has, as it were, a built-in imperative to select as one's "supreme end" the good of God and his universe, for this universal benevolence is an exercise of one's highest powers, which have priority over all others. Hopkins wrote:

> In seeking the foundation of obligation, I suppose moral beings to exist. As having intelligence and sensibility I suppose them capable of apprehending ends good in themselves, and an end thus that is both ultimate and supreme. In the apprehension of such an end I suppose the moral reason must affirm obligation to choose it, and that all acts that will, of their nature, lead to the attainment of this end, are right. [*Law of Love, and Love as a Law*, 1869, p. 26]

The teleological moralists, among whom are to be included (beside Hopkins) Charles G. Finney, James H. Fairchild, Wiliam A. Smith, and Noah Porter, began, humanely enough, with man as he is—or as they believed him to be. They were, however, open to criticism on logical grounds for taking an illegitimate step from descriptive statements about human psychology to imperative judgments about moral duty. It may be true that the greatest enjoyment comes from doing good for others; but is it permissible to draw the conclusion that, therefore, one *ought* to do good for others? As Joseph Haven maintained, there is no logical reason to insert "therefore" between the propositions "I perceive such a course of action to be conducive to happiness" and "I am under obligation to pursue that course" (*Moral Philosophy*, 1859, p. 23).

Deontological ethics or, as they were called at the time, "rightarian" ethics avoid this kind of difficulty. It is assumed at the outset that "duty" is a simple, indefinable notion—the other side of the coin of "right." Once it is agreed that a course of action is right, to ask why one ought to pursue it seems logically gratuitous. Deontological theorists like Haven were critical of utilitarians who attempted to justify obligation. The answer to the question "*Why* ought?" is obvious, he said: "We ought *because it is right*." Haven insisted that the "term *right* expresses a simple and ultimate idea." It is, therefore, "incapable of analysis and definition." Although "right" and "duty" are "not precisely synonymous terms," he maintained, they are "nearly equivalent." Right is the "*foundation* of obligation, and coextensive with it." And duty is the right as it presents itself to moral agents (*Moral Philosophy*, pp. 21–23).

The main problem facing the deontological theorist is not that of justifying obligation but that of determining what is right. The idea of right is purely formal, and the distinction between right and wrong is as empty of content as that between A and not-A. The question, therefore, becomes one of knowledge: that is, "How is one to determine which moral rules (or what actions) are right under the circumstances?" Thus, while teleological moralists, in their attempts to define the good and to establish duty, usually move toward utilitarianism and either hedonism or sentimentalism, deontological moralists, in trying to explain our knowledge of an indefinable right, tend to become intuitionists.

Those American academic moralists who held a deontological theory of ethics were divided into two groups in their ethical epistemology. Some held that right is known in itself, that the conscience both recognizes the authority of the right in some formal sense and informs us of our duty in specific cases. This position was held by Haven, Archibald Alexander, and Francis Bowen, all of whom held that we become aware of moral "laws" only as the conscience judges specific actions—much as the senses perceive certain facts. On the basis of these specific judgments, we make generalizations about the content of the moral law: like a scientist organizing his data, we proceed inductively toward increasingly abstract rules and principles, gradually outlining the dimensions of the moral law. Others, however, held that we intuitively apprehend the rightness not of specific acts but of certain rules that legitimately govern us in our relations with others. Thus, we no sooner think of the relation of the child to its parent than our minds are presented with particular attitudes and forms of behavior that are morally appropriate to that relationship—the duty of a child to respect and obey its parent, or that of the parent to protect and educate its child. Variations of this position were held by Wayland, Mahan, and Peabody. In any given relation, personal, political, or religious, there is a course of action that is right or "fitting." Our *prima-facie* obligation is established once this relation and its moral significance are understood.

Each of these deontological positions has its limitations. Deontological theories that concentrate on specific acts can provide an excuse for moral relativism. For if the final authority in morality is the intuitive judgment of the conscience in any given situation, there is theoretically no way of refuting someone's mistaken or arbitrary moral judgment. In a different way, those deontological theories that employ general rules also provide no standard by which to order moral priorities when several rules apply and come into mutual conflict. To overcome these deficiencies Wayland, for example, made a teleological appeal to prudence and, like most of the other proponents of the "rightarian" position, relied on divine revelation to supplement intuition. In fact, the secret weapon of all the academic moralists was the appeal to Scripture and, more broadly, to God's moral law, however it might be apprehended. Although they dealt dutifully with the logic of ethics, and realized that God's naked will is no proper basis for a rational theory of duty, they all relied ultimately on their faith that God's will and the moral law coincide. This point of view was perhaps most clearly expressed by John Leadley Dagg, who argued that, even though moral distinctions are independent of God's will (they are expressive of his "nature"), our duty—so far as we can know it in this life—is known only through the revealed

161

"will of God" (*Elements of Moral Science*, 1859, pp. 91–96). When all the ethical arguments had been presented, criticized, defended, revised, and abandoned, man would remain—as he always has been—the child of a righteous God to whom he owes final and everlasting obedience.

Acknowledgments

In the course of preparing my book I received generous help from many. Wilson Smith, whose study *Professors and Public Ethics* (1956) provided a good starting point for my own research, kindly took the time at an early stage to give me many useful suggestions, and gave my completed manuscript a close and critical reading. Professors Ernest Lee Tuveson, Charles G. Sellers, and William R. Dennes offered sound advice and welcome encouragement; and Professor Herbert W. Schneider was most helpful in making suggestions for revision and clarification. I have gratefully received the criticism and suggestions of Jason Cain, John Welles Gould, Tai Liu, Peter G. Slater, and Raymond Wolters, and am particularly in debt to Daniel Walker Howe, who read and reread various versions of my manuscript, exposed all too many shortcomings, and proposed many new lines of inquiry. The University of California and the University of Delaware were both generous with research and fellowship funds, and the library staffs of both institutions were extremely co-operative, patient, and, when necessary, commiserating.

My greatest debt, intellectual and moral, is to Henry F. May, who was there from the start, remained with me every step of the way, and shared all the agonies attending the preparation and revision of a manuscript. Henry May has provided a model of scholarly discipline and intellectual

Acknowledgments

honesty to live up to. More than this, he has been a friend.

Finally, there is Mimi, my wife, who lived it, and whose warmth and ready affection always reminded me that there is more—much more—to life than the Science of Morals.

D. H. Meyer

Newark, Delaware

Notes

Introduction

1. John Dewey, "From Absolutism to Experimentalism," *Contemporary American Philosophy: Personal Statements*, George P. Adams and William P. Montague, ed. (two volumes; New York, 1930), II, 13.
2. Ralph Waldo Emerson, "The Present State of Ethical Philosophy," Bowdoin Prize Essay, 1821. In Kenneth Walter Cameron, ed., *Transcendental Climate: New Resources for the Study of Emerson, Thoreau and Their Contemporaries* (three volumes; Hartford, 1963), I, esp. pp. 15–19.
3. George P. Schmidt, *The Old Time College President* (New York, 1930), pp. 108–45.
4. Article on "Moral Philosophy," by Francis Lieber, *Encyclopaedia Americana* (revised edition; Philadelphia, 1849), IX, 31–33.
5. John Witherspoon, *Lectures on Moral Philosophy* (Princeton, 1912; first published, 1800), pp. 1–2. On the rise of moral philosophy from "the fringes of Puritan respectability" to prominence in the eighteenth century, see Norman S. Fiering, "President Samuel Johnson and the Circle of Knowledge," *William and Mary Quarterly*, 28, ser. 3 (1971), 199–236.
6. Charles Sanders Peirce, "The Fixation of Belief," *Popular Science Monthly*, 12 (1877), 1–15.
7. William James, letter to Charles Renouvier, August 5, 1883. In *The Letters of William James*, Henry James, ed.

165

(two volumes; Boston, 1920), I, 231. James was writing with reference to Noah Porter of Yale.

8. Schmidt, *Old Time College President*, pp. 143–45.

Chapter 1

1. Philip Schaff, *America* (New York, 1855), p. 43.
2. *Ibid.;* Francis Grund, *The Americans in Their Moral, Social, and Political Relations* (two volumes; London, 1837), I, 298.
3. Horace Mann, "The Necessity of Education in a Republican Government" (1839), *Lectures on Education* (Boston, 1850), p. 124. See also Rush Welter, *Popular Education and Democratic Thought in America* (New York and London, 1962), pp. 45–137.
4. Stow Persons, *American Minds: A History of Ideas* (New York, 1958), p. 189. On the old-time college see also: Schmidt, *Old Time College President;* Donald Tewksbury, *The Founding of American Colleges and Universities before the Civil War* (New York, 1932); Richard Hofstadter, *Academic Freedom in the Age of the College* (New York, 1955), Chapter V; Frederick Rudolph, *The American College and University* (New York, 1962); Laurence R. Veysey, *The Emergence of the American University* (Chicago and London, 1965), pp. 21–56; and Oscar and Mary Handlin, *The American College and American Culture* (New York, 1970), pp. 19–42.
5. Noah Porter, "On Moral Science, as a Branch of Academical Education," *Quarterly Christian Spectator*, 6, ser. 3 (1834), 561–80.
6. *Ibid.*, p. 576.
7. Persons, *American Minds*, p. 189.
8. See Ralph Henry Gabriel, *Religion and Learning at Yale* (New Haven, 1958), pp. 100–108.
9. Walter Houghton, *The Victorian Frame of Mind, 1830–1870* (New Haven, 1957), pp. 10–11.
10. Mark Hopkins, *The Law of Love and Love as a Law; Or, Moral Science, Theoretical and Practical* (New York, 1869), p. 10.
11. Schmidt, *Old Time College President*, p. 109.
12. Thomas Clap, *An Essay on the Nature and Foundation of Moral Virtue and Obligation; Being a Short Introduction to the Study of Ethics; For the Use of Students at Yale Col-*

lege (New Haven, 1765). Other early American writers on moral philosophy include Samuel Johnson and John Daniel Gros, of Columbia, and John Witherspoon and Samuel Stanhope Smith, of Princeton. For a recent examination of the subject see Norman Fiering, "Moral Philosophy in America, 1650–1750, and Its British Context" (unpublished doctoral dissertation, Columbia University, 1969).

13. See Wilson Smith, *Professors and Public Ethics: Studies of Northern Moral Philosophers before the Civil War* (Ithaca, New York, 1956), pp. 44–73, and Wendell Glick, "Bishop [*sic*] Paley in America," *New England Quarterly*, 27 (1954), 345–54.

14. Smith, *Professors and Public Ethics*, pp. 44–63, argues that Paley's utilitarian moral theory was extremely influential in America in the first quarter of the nineteenth century. I would maintain that, although Paley's text on moral philosophy was widely used, there is little evidence to support the conclusion that his moral theory was ever widely accepted.

15. See, for example, Noah Porter, "On Moral Science," *loc. cit.;* Archibald Alexander, review of Wayland's *Moral Science*, in *The Princeton Review and Biblical Repository*, 7, ser. 2 (1835), 377–79, 388–89; Francis Bowen, review of Wayland's *Moral Science*, *The Christian Examiner*, 22 (1837), 365–68; and Jasper Adams, *Elements of Moral Philosophy* (Philadelphia, 1837), p. xii.

16. William Paley, *Principles of Moral and Political Philosophy* (London, 1785), in *The Works of William Paley, D.D.* (Philadelphia, 1831), p. 34.

17. *Ibid.*, pp. 36–37.

18. *Ibid.*, p. 37.

19. Smith, *Professors and Public Ethics*, pp. 187–88, 198–201.

20. American moral philosophers often referred to Paley by name in refuting his system, although sometimes they argued against utilitarianism generally. See, for example, Francis Wayland, *Elements of Moral Science* (1835), Joseph L. Blau, ed. (Cambridge, Massachusetts, 1963), pp. 29–36; Francis Bowen, *Critical Essays on a Few Subjects Connected with the History and Present Condition of Speculative Philosophy* (Boston, 1842), pp. 167–70;

Charles G. Finney, *Lectures on Systematic Theology* (two volumes; Oberlin, 1846, 1847), I, 127–38; Archibald Alexander, *Outlines of Moral Science* (New York, 1852), pp. 19–33; Hopkins, *Law of Love*, pp. 19–33; John Leadley Dagg, *Elements of Moral Science* (New York, 1859), pp. 38–39; Joseph Haven, *Moral Philosophy* (New York, 1880; 1859), pp. 39–45.

21. Jay Wharton Fay, *American Psychology before William James* (New Brunswick, New Jersey, 1939), pp. 90 ff., has noted a parallel development in the related area of psychology (mental science), beginning in the late 1820's.

22. Wayland, *Moral Science*, p. 3. Cf. Mark Hopkins, *Lectures on Moral Science, Delivered before the Lowell Institute, Boston* (Boston, 1862), p. viii.

23. See Alexander's and Bowen's reviews of Wayland's text, *loc. cit.*, and Francis (Jr.) and H. L. Wayland, *A Memoir of the Life and Labors of Francis Wayland, D.D., LL.D.* (two volumes; New York, 1867), I, 383 ff.

24. Asa Burton, for instance, in his *Essays on Some of the First Principles of Metaphysicks, Ethicks, and Theology* (Portland, Maine, 1824), had dealt with conscience and the problem of moral distinctions; but he had shown little concern with the problem of moral obligation and little recognition of the special quality of moral concepts.

25. Wayland, *Moral Science*, p. 3.

26. Fiering, "Samuel Johnson," *loc. cit.*, p. 233.

27. Bowen, review of Wayland, *loc. cit.*, pp. 365–66.

Chapter 2

1. See Theodore Collier's biographical sketch in the *Dictionary of American Biography* and Smith, *Professors and Public Ethics*, pp. 128–46. On Wayland's moral theory see Edward H. Madden, *Civil Disobedience and Moral Law in Nineteenth-Century Moral Philosophy* (Seattle and London, 1968), pp. 16–43. Wayland, *Memoir*, is laudatory but contains useful excerpts from Wayland's journals.

2. See Wayland's *Thoughts on the Present Collegiate System in the United States* (Boston, 1842) and his *Report to the Corporation of Brown University on Changes in the System of Collegiate Education* (Providence, 1850).

3. Joseph L. Blau, "Introduction" to the 1963 edition of Wayland's *Moral Science*, p. xlii.

4. Letter of July 9, 1861; in Wayland, *Memoir*, I, 125.

5. Francis Wayland, *Salvation by Christ* (Boston, 1859), p. 35.
6. Wayland, *Moral Science*, pp. 37–41.
7. Bowen, review of Wayland, *loc. cit.*, pp. 373–82.
8. Wayland, *Moral Science*, pp. 138–49.
9. See Wayland's sermon on the subject in his *Sermons to the Churches* (New York, Boston, London, 1858), pp. 144–77.
10. *Ibid.*, p. v.
11. Francis Wayland, *Limitations of Human Responsibility* (Boston, 1838), p. 8.
12. The most recent and best monograph on Hopkins is Frederick Rudolph, *Mark Hopkins and the Log: Williams College, 1836–1872* (New Haven, 1956), which concentrates on Hopkins as educator. See also William W. Fenn's sketch of Hopkins in the *Dictionary of American Biography*.
13. John Hopkins Denison, *Mark Hopkins: A Biography* (New York, 1935), p. 147.
14. Quoted in Rudolph, *Hopkins*, p. 27.
15. This letter is reproduced in George S. Merriam, ed., *Noah Porter: A Memorial by Friends* (New York, 1893), pp. 184–85.
16. Rudolph, *Hopkins*, p. 28.
17. G. Stanley Hall, "Philosophy in the United States," *Mind*, 4 (1879), 93.
18. Hopkins, *Moral Science*, p. vii.
19. *Ibid.*, pp. 49–58.
20. *Ibid.*, pp. 259–60; *Law of Love*, pp. 289–96.
21. See Francis Bowen, *Principles of Political Economy Applied to the Condition, the Resources, and the Institutions of the American People* (Boston, 1856); and his *Lowell Lectures on the Application of Metaphysical and Ethical Sciences to the Evidences of Religion* (Boston, 1849).
22. See Ernest Sutherland Bates's biographical essay on Bowen in the *Dictionary of American Biography*.
23. Bowen collected many of these reviews in his *Critical Essays*.
24. Sydney Ahlstrom, "The Middle Period (1840–80)," *The Harvard Divinity School: Its Place in Harvard University and in American Culture*, George H. Williams, ed. (Boston, 1954), p. 88.
25. See Conrad Wright, *The Beginnings of Unitarianism in America* (Boston, 1955).

26. Clarence H. Faust, "The Background of the Unitarian Opposition to Transcendentalism," *Modern Philology*, 35 (1938), 297–324.

27. This rapprochement is discussed by Timothy L. Smith, *Revivalism and Social Reform in Mid-Nineteenth-Century America* (New York and Nashville, 1957), pp. 95–102. On the conservative Unitarian world-view see O. B. Frothingham, *Boston Unitarianism, 1820–1850* (New York, 1890), and particularly Daniel Walker Howe, *The Unitarian Conscience: Harvard Moral Philosophy, 1805–1861* (Cambridge, Massachusetts, 1970).

28. Bowen, review of Wayland, p. 381.

29. Bowen, *Lowell Lectures*, p. 45.

30. *Ibid.*, p. 290; see pp. 288–322.

31. See Howe, *Unitarian Conscience*, p. 102.

32. Richard Hildreth, one of Bowen's least friendly critics, offered a brilliant analysis of the dilemma of Christian ethics in his "Joint Letter to Orestes A. Brownson and the Editor of the 'North American Review': In Which the Editor of the North American Review is Proved to Be No Christian and Little Better Than an Atheist," in Martha M. Pingel, ed., *An American Utilitarian: Richard Hildreth as a Philosopher* (New York, 1948), pp. 153–76.

33. A sketch of Alexander's life by Frederick W. Loetscher appears in the *Dictionary of American Biography*. The intellectual milieu at Princeton in the late eighteenth century is reconstructed by Douglas Sloan, *The Scottish Enlightenment and the American College Ideal* (New York, 1971).

34. Alexander, *Moral Science*, p. 12.

35. *Ibid.*, pp. 19–88, 141–208, 253–55.

36. *Ibid.*, pp. 89–146.

37. See Hopkins, *Law of Love*, pp. 99–117, and Wayland, *Moral Science*, pp. 174–81, 339–44. See also William K. Frankena, "Foreword" to his edition of Jonathan Edwards, *Nature of True Virtue* (Ann Arbor, 1960).

38. Madden, *Civil Disobedience*, pp. 20–22.

Chapter 3

1. On the importance of distinguishing between (the process of) thinking and (the product of) thought in intellectual history, see Joseph Levenson, *Confucian China and Its*

Modern Fate, Vol. I: *The Problem of Intellectual Continuity* (Berkeley and Los Angeles, 1958), esp. pp. xiii–xix,
212.

2. William Warren Sweet, *The Story of Religion in America*
   (revised edition; New York, 1950), pp. 258–84.
3. Smith, *Revivalism and Social Reform*, pp. 32–33.
4. See: Sidney E. Mead, *Nathaniel William Taylor, 1786–
   1858: A Connecticut Liberal* (Chicago, 1942); Barbara
   M. Cross, *Horace Bushnell: Minister to a Changing
   America* (Chicago, 1958); and William G. McLoughlin,
   *The Meaning of Henry Ward Beecher: An Essay on the
   Shifting Values of Mid-Victorian America, 1840–1870*
   (New York, 1970). See also Sidney E. Mead, *The Lively
   Experiment: The Shaping of Christianity in America* (New
   York, Evanston, London, 1963), pp. 103–55.
5. *Lowell Lectures*, p. 42.
6. Adams, *Moral Philosophy*, p. 71.
7. *Ibid.*, p. 66.
8. For example see Mark Hopkins's "Introduction" to Emerson Davis, *The Half-Century or, a History of the Changes
   That Have Taken Place, and Events That Have Transpired, Chiefly in the United States, between 1800 and
   1850* (Boston, 1851).
9. Henri Bergson, *The Two Sources of Morality and Religion*,
   tr. R. A. Audra and Cloudsley Brereton (New York,
   1935), Chapter I.
10. See Richard Chase, *The Democratic Vista: A Dialogue on
    Life and Letters in Contemporary America* (New York,
    1958), pp. 120–66. On the three kinds of American con-
    servatism see: Allen Guttmann, *The Conservative Tra-
    dition in America* (New York, 1967), on Burkean
    conservatism; Robert G. McCloskey, *American Conserva-
    tism in an Age of Enterprise, 1865–1910* (Cambridge,
    Massachusetts, 1951), for American Whiggish conserva-
    tism; and Richard Hofstadter, *The Paranoid Style in
    American Politics and Other Essays* (New York, 1967),
    Part I, for what is frequently called "pseudo-conservatism."
11. William Wilberforce, *A Practical View of the Prevailing
    Religious System of Professed Christians, in the Higher
    and Middle Classes, Contrasted with Real Christianity*
    (fourth American edition; Boston, 1815), pp. 140–41,
    199, 204, 238.

12. William Andrew Smith, *Lectures on the Philosophy and Practice of Slavery, as Exhibited in the Institution of Domestic Slavery in the United States: With the Duties of Masters to Slaves* (Nashville, 1856), p. 90.

Chapter 4

1. Witherspoon, *Moral Philosophy*, p. 4.
2. For some explicit statements see Adams, *Moral Philosophy*, pp. 1–2; Haven, *Moral Philosophy*, pp. 15–17, where he insists, however, that moral philosophy cannot be reduced to mental science; and Hopkins, *Moral Science*, pp. 79–101.
3. See Herbert W. Schneider, *A History of American Philosophy* (New York, 1946), p. 241.
4. Cited in Joseph L. Blau, *Men and Movements in American Philosophy* (New York, 1952), pp. 105–108. On Bowen's early commitment to the Scottish philosophy see Howe, *Unitarian Conscience*, pp. 80–81.
5. James McCosh, *The Scottish Philosophy, Biographical, Expository, Critical, from Hutcheson to Hamilton* (New York, 1875), pp. 2–7, 68–69. See also Thomas Temund Jessop, *A Bibliography of David Hume and of Scottish Philosophy from Francis Hutcheson to Lord Balfour* (London, 1938), pp. v–ix.
6. Francis Hutcheson, *Inquiry into the Original of Our Ideas of Beauty and Virtue* (London, 1725), sections I and II. See also, *Essays on the Nature and Conduct of the Passions with Illustrations from the Moral Sense* (London, 1728).
7. On Hutcheson's influence on Hume see Norman Kemp Smith, *The Philosophy of David Hume: A Critical Study of Its Origins and Its Central Doctrines* (London, 1941), esp. pp. 24–41. On his influence in colonial America see Fiering, "Moral Philosophy in America." For some nineteenth-century American criticisms of Hutcheson's moral theory, see, besides McCosh, *Scottish Philosophy*, pp. 84–86, Dagg, *Moral Science*, pp. 34–36, and Noah Porter, *Elements of Moral Science, Theoretical and Practical* (New York, 1884), pp. 135–36, 181–83.
8. McCosh, *Scottish Philosophy*, p. 192. S. A. Grave, *The Scottish Philosophy of Common Sense* (Oxford, 1960), pp. 6–7, regards Reid as the founder of the "common-sense" school of Scottish philosophy.

9. Emerson, "Present State of Ethical Philosophy," *loc. cit.*, I, 19.
10. David Hume, *A Treatise of Human Nature* (1739), L. A. Selby-Bigge, ed. (Oxford, 1888), pp. 103, 118–23. On Hume's extension of Hutcheson's interpretation, see Smith, *Philosophy of David Hume*, pp. 47, 73. Locke treats "The Reality of Knowledge" in his *Essay Concerning Human Understanding*, Alexander Campbell Fraser, ed. (two volumes; New York, 1959), II, 226–43. Locke's *Essay* first appeared in 1680; the Fraser edition was first published in 1894.
11. Thomas Reid, *An Inquiry into the Human Mind, On the Principles of Common Sense* (second edition; London, 1765), pp. 2–4.
12. For more detail see Grave, *Scottish Philosophy*, esp. pp. 82–189, and Timothy Duggan's introduction to his edition of Reid's *Inquiry* (Chicago and London, 1970).
13. Reid, *Inquiry*, pp. 288–354. Reid's criticism of Lockean empiricism is treated sympathetically by David Daiches Raphael, *The Moral Sense* (Oxford, 1947), pp. 148–51.
14. Reid, *Inquiry*, p. 378.
15. James Beattie, *An Essay on the Nature and Immutability of Truth, in Opposition to Sophistry and Skepticism* (sixth edition; Edinburgh, 1805; first edition, 1770), p. 21.
16. *Ibid.*, pp. 9–10.
17. Reid's debt to Butler for his "moral psychology" is discussed by Henry Sidgwick, *Outlines of the History of Ethics* (Boston, 1960; first published, 1886), pp. 226–29. Butler's position is spelled out in his *Fifteen Sermons Preached at the Rolls Chapel* (London, 1726).
18. Thomas Reid, *Essays on the Active Powers of Man* (1788); in the *Works of Thomas Reid, D.D.*, Sir William Hamilton, ed. (Edinburgh, 1863), II, 592–94, 670–79.
19. *Ibid.*, pp. 594–99, 638.
20. *Ibid.*, p. 581.
21. For Price's position see his *Review of the Principal Questions in Morals* (1758; enlarged, 1781), D. D. Raphael, ed. (London, 1948). Similarities and differences between Reid and Price are treated in Raphael, *Moral Sense*, pp. 148–51, and in Torgny T. Segerstedt, *The Problem of Knowledge in Scottish Philosophy* (Lund, 1935), pp. 31–34.

22. Reid, *Active Powers, Works*, II, 579–99.
23. See Grave, *Scottish Philosophy*, pp. 229–40.
24. Dugald Stewart, *Philosophy of the Active and Moral Powers of Man* (two volumes; Edinburgh, 1828); in Sir William Hamilton, ed., *The Collected Works of Dugald Stewart, Esq.*, F.R.S.S. (Edinburgh and Boston, 1855), VI, 295–301, 318–26; VII, 351–53.
25. *Ibid.*, VI, 278.
26. James Walker, ed., *Stewart's Philosophy of the Active and Moral Powers of Man* (one-volume abridgement; Cambridge, Massachusetts, 1849).
27. According to McCosh, *Scottish Philosophy*, pp. 8–9, the common-sense philosophy had wide influence throughout the western world. The influence of the Scottish philosophy in the United States has been much discussed. In American theology, see Sydney Ahlstrom, "The Scottish Philosophy and American Theology," *Church History*, 24 (1955), 257–72. In literature and criticism see William Charvat, *The Origins of American Critical Thought, 1810–1835* (Philadelphia, 1936), Chapter III, and Terence Martin, *The Instructed Vision: Scottish Common Sense Philosophy and the Origins of American Fiction* (Bloomington, Indiana, 1961). In philosophy, besides Schneider, *History of American Philosophy*, pp. 246–50, see I. Woodbridge Riley, *American Philosophy, the Early Schools* (New York, 1907), pp. 475–563. As far as the old-time college is concerned, see George P. Schmidt, *The Liberal Arts College* (New Brunswick, New Jersey, 1957), pp. 46–51, and Douglas Sloan, *The Scottish Enlightenment and the American College Ideal.*

Chapter 5

1. G. Stanley Hall, "On the History of American College Textbooks and Teaching in Logic, Ethics, Psychology and Allied Subjects," American Antiquarian Society, *Proceedings*, 9, ser. 2 (1894), 152.
2. Reid was particularly concerned to maintain the mind-matter dualism. See his *Essay on the Intellectual Powers of Man* (1785) in Reid, *Works*, I, 236–38. Virtually all the American moral philosophers considered in this study insisted on the mind-matter dualism. For some explicit statements see: Asa Mahan, *Abstract of a Course of Lectures on Mental and Moral Philosophy* (Oberlin, 1840), p. 9;

Wayland, *Elements of Intellectual Philosophy* (revised edition; New York, 1865), pp. 9–13; Andrew Preston Peabody, *Christian Morals; A Series of Lectures* (Boston, 1887), pp. 137–38. For a discussion of "The Psychologizing of Philosophy," with reference to Noah Porter, see Joseph L. Blau, *Men and Movements*, pp. 102–109.

3. For examples see Francis Wayland, "A Discourse on the Philosophy of Analogy," 1831; and Noah Porter, "The Science of Nature versus the Science of Man; A Plea for the Science of Man," 1871. Both are reproduced in Joseph L. Blau, ed., *American Philosophic Addresses, 1700–1900* (New York, 1946), pp. 347–63, 457–86.

4. See the "Author's Introduction" to Butler, *Analogy of Religion* (London, 1736). See also Leslie Stephen, *History of English Thought in the Eighteenth Century* (London, 1876), Chapter V.

5. Wayland, *Moral Science*, p. 4. See also Joseph Blau's introduction, pp. xxii–xxix.

6. *Ibid.*, pp. 42–63, 367–70.

7. *Ibid.*, pp. 43–44.

8. *Ibid.*, p. 63.

9. Wayland, *Intellectual Philosophy*, pp. 136–42.

10. Wayland, *Moral Science*, pp. 367–70.

11. *Ibid.*, pp. 100–106. See also Madden, *Civil Disobedience*, pp. 20–22.

12. Wayland, *Moral Science*, p. 100.

13. Wayland, *Human Responsibility*, p. 8.

14. Wayland, *Moral Science*, pp. 42–43. Francis Bowen, Jasper Adams, James McCosh, Archibald Alexander, James Walker, Andrew Preston Peabody, and Wayland were all inclined to consider conscience a separate faculty. Asa Mahan, Charles G. Finney, James H. Fairchild, John L. Dagg, Joseph Haven, Mark Hopkins, and Noah Porter argued the contrary, using "conscience" to refer to a particular operation of the reason or, jointly, of the reason and the sensibility.

15. Hopkins, *Moral Science*, pp. 176, 205–27. See also his *Law of Love*, pp. 90–98.

16. Finney, *Systematic Theology*, I, 30–31; Porter, *Moral Science*, pp. 245–49, 253–55.

17. Asa Mahan, *Science of Moral Philosophy* (Oberlin, 1848), pp. 24–41. Mahan's treatment in his earlier *Abstract*, pp. 189–202, 212–20, was less satisfactory.

18. See, for example, Bowen, *Lowell Lectures*, pp. 266–89, 298–302; Alexander, *Moral Science*, pp. 18–88, 188–89; Adams, *Moral Philosophy*, pp. 14–29; Haven, *Moral Philosophy*, pp. 15–17; James McCosh, *Method of the Divine Government Physical and Moral* (London, 1883; first published, 1850), pp. 291–307.
19. Alexander, *Moral Science*, pp. 48–50, 64–77, 86, 188–89, 255.
20. Wayland, *Moral Science*, p. 53.
21. Alexander, *Moral Science*, p. 86.
22. Bowen, *Lowell Lectures*, pp. 301–302.
23. Mahan, *Moral Philosophy*, pp. 154–55.
24. McCosh, *Divine Government*, p. 325.
25. John Dewey, "From Absolutism to Experimentalism," *loc. cit.*, p. 15.

Chapter 6

1. Immanuel Kant, *Foundations of the Metaphysics of Morals* (1785), tr. Lewis White Beck (Indianapolis and New York, 1959), p. 9.
2. Thomas Sprat, *History of the Royal Society* (second edition; London, 1702), pp. 111–12.
3. See Calvin's *Institutes of the Christian Religion* (1536–56), Book II, Chapters II–V. See also Herschel Baker, *The Image of Man: A Study of the Idea of Human Dignity in Classical Antiquity, the Middle Ages, and the Renaissance* (New York, 1961; first published, 1947), pp. 318–22.
4. Jonathan Edwards, *A Careful and Strict Enquiry into the Modern Prevailing Notions of that Freedom of Will, Which is Supposed to Be Essential to Moral Agency, Vertue and Vice, Reward and Punishment, Praise and Blame* (Boston, 1754), in Paul Ramsey, ed., *The Works of Jonathan Edwards* (New Haven, 1957), I, 137–48.
5. Edwards's continuing influence is treated in Frank Hugh Foster, *Genetic History of the New England Theology* (Chicago, 1907).
6. Edwards, *Freedom of Will, Works*, I, 172–74.
7. *Ibid.*, pp. 139–67.
8. Henry Tappan, *A Review of Edwards's "Inquiry into the Freedom of the Will"* (New York, 1839), pp. iii, viii.
9. See Thomas Reid, *Active Powers, Works*, II, 531. Reid

had early distinguished between the volitions and the affections. The French Eclectics of the early nineteenth century, Victor Cousin and his disciple Théodore Jouffroy, were much infatuated with the psychologism of the Scottish philosophy, and further developed many of the ideas of Reid and Dugald Stewart. The influence of the French school in America is discussed by William Henry Channing in his preface to Jouffroy's *Introduction to Ethics, Including a Critical Survey of Moral Systems*, tr. W. H. Channing (two volumes; Boston and Cambridge, 1838), I, vii-xix.

10. Finney, *Systematic Theology*, I, 210; 25–27.
11. Calvin, *Institutes*, Bk. I, Ch. XV, nos. vi–viii.
12. Alexander, *Moral Science*, pp. 89–100, 111.
13. *Ibid.*, pp. 113, 208.
14. *Ibid.*, pp. 141–58, 199–208.
15. See, for example, Wayland's sermons on "The Moral Character of Man," *Salvation by Christ*, pp. 31–79; Finney, *Systematic Theology*, II, 11–64, 245–318; and James Walker, *Sermons Preached Chiefly in the College Chapel* (two volumes; Boston, 1892), II, 295–96.
16. McCosh, *Divine Government*, p. 285.
17. Alexander, *Moral Science*, p. 99.
18. See, for example, Jacob Haroutunian, *Piety versus Moralism: The Passing of the New England Theology* (New York, 1932); Sidney E. Mead, *Nathaniel William Taylor*, esp. pp. 95–127; Sydney Ahlstrom, "The Scottish Philosophy in American Theology," *loc. cit.*, pp. 257–72; and Stow Persons, *American Minds*, pp. 172–77.
19. See Jonathan Edwards, *Nature of True Virtue* (1765), William K. Frankena, ed. (Ann Arbor, 1960), pp. 1–13, 42–60. This theme was developed further by the followers of Edwards, including Nathaniel William Taylor, *Lectures on the Moral Government of God* (two volumes; New York, 1859), I, 18–30. See also Finney, *Systematic Theology*, I, 26–34, 157, 163, 209–13; II, 78–95, 187–203; and Hopkins, *Moral Science*, pp. 162–73, and *Law of Love*, pp. 40–46.
20. Wayland, *Moral Science*, pp. 25–26.
21. Robert Baird, *Religion in America* (New York, 1844), p. 290.
22. Finney, *Systematic Theology*, II, 11–64; Mahan, *Moral Philosophy*, pp. 63–69.

23. Adams, *Moral Philosophy*, pp. 1–2.
24. This is a matter of emphasis rather than of explicit statement, and it is difficult to document. For some representative discussions of man's moral powers, particularly the proper function of the will, appetites, and sensibilities, see: Finney, *Systematic Theology*, I, 25–33; Mahan, *Abstract*, pp. 29–31; Bowen, *Lowell Lectures*, pp. 222–65; McCosh, *Moral Government*, pp. 262–86; Haven, *Moral Philosophy*, pp. 59–70; Hopkins, *Moral Science*, pp. 129–92.

Chapter 7

1. Bowen, *Lowell Lectures*, pp. xii–xiii.
2. Hopkins, *Law of Love*, pp. 129–31; *Moral Science*, pp. 59–78.
3. Both Francis Wayland and John Leadley Dagg said essentially the same thing as Hopkins. See Wayland, *Moral Science*, pp. 89–99; and Dagg, *Moral Science*, pp. 89–91.
4. For some representative discussions see Adams, *Moral Philosophy*, pp. 271–308; Dagg, *Moral Science*, pp. 303–19; and Haven, *Moral Philosophy*, pp. 99–102.
5. Edward Everett, *Orations and Speeches on Various Occasions* (two volumes; Boston, 1853), II, 493–518; Walker, sermon on "Character" (n.d.), *Sermons*, I, 116–23.
6. See Schmidt, *Old Time College President;* and Veysey, *Emergence of the American University*, pp. 21–56.
7. Stephen Olin, "Formation of Character in College" (n.d.), in *Works of Stephen Olin, D.D., LL.D.* (two volumes; New York, 1854), II, 94–104.
8. Asa Mahan, *Autobiography: Intellectual, Moral, and Spiritual* (London, 1882), pp. 252, 263–65.
9. The relation between mental discipline and the faculty psychology is discussed by Walter B. Kolesnik, *Mental Discipline in Modern Education* (Madison, 1958), pp. 6, 89–112. Even those moral philosophers, like John Leadley Dagg, who insisted strongly on the unity of the mind, fell into the habit of speaking of the "faculties."
10. Olin, "Formation of Character," pp. 55–56, 103–104. See also Mark Hopkins, *An Address Delivered in Boston, May 26, 1852* (Boston, 1852), pp. 7–9; and Walker, *Sermons*, II, 323–39.
11. Hopkins, *Moral Science*, p. 177. See also Walker, *Sermons*, I, 285.

12. See Robert S. Fletcher, *A History of Oberlin College from Its Foundation through the Civil War* (two volumes; Oberlin, 1943), II, 701; and Thomas LeDuc, *Piety and Intellect at Amherst College, 1865–1912* (New York, 1946), pp. 30–33.

13. Finney, *Systematic Theology*, II, 197–203. For a similar point of view see Hopkins, *Moral Science*, pp. 39–58, 154–55, 165–66, and Porter, *Moral Science*, pp. 96–111.

14. William James, *Principles of Psychology* (two volumes; New York, 1890), I, 125, 126. James' chapter on habit had been published in 1887 in the *Popular Science Monthly*. See also John Dewey's discussion of moral control in his *Psychology* (third revised edition, 1891; first edition, 1887) in *Dewey's Early Works, 1882–1898*, George E. Axtelle, *et al.*, ed. (Carbondale and Edwardsville, 1967), II, 342–56.

Chapter 8

1. Adams, *Moral Philosophy*, p. x. Gladys Bryson, *Man and Society: The Scottish Inquiry of the Eighteenth Century* (Princeton, 1945), p. 177, discusses this practice among eighteenth-century Scottish moralists.

2. See, for example, Wayland, *Moral Science*, pp. 188–94; Hopkins, *Moral Science*, pp. 258–60; and Haven, *Moral Philosophy*, pp. 118–42.

3. Smith, *Professors and Public Ethics*, p. 35.

4. Wayland, *Moral Science*, pp. 89–99.

5. *Ibid.*, pp. 174–81, 339–44.

6. Adams, *Moral Philosophy*, pp. 270–304.

7. See Joseph Butler, Dissertation II, "Of the Nature of Virtue," appended to his *Analogy of Religion*, esp. pp. 462–67. Butler was reacting against moralists like Francis Hutcheson who identified virtue with benevolence.

8. See Stewart, *Active and Moral Powers of Man, Works*, VII, 276–78, 351–66. On the importance of distinguishing between virtue and duty, see Henry Sidgwick, *Methods of Ethics* (Chicago, 1962; seventh revised edition, 1902), pp. 217–30.

9. Immanuel Kant, *The Doctrine of Virtue*, tr. Mary J. Gregor (Philadelphia, 1971; first published in German, 1797), pp. 290–305.

10. Wayland, *Moral Science*, pp. 254–64.

11. Mahan, *Moral Philosophy*, pp. 223–24.
12. Haven, *Moral Philosophy*, pp. 21–50, 325–58.
13. Kant, *Doctrine of Virtue*, pp. 161–67, argues that pure moral philosophy cannot accommodate the doctrine of duties to God, and his reasoning seems irrefutable.
14. Hopkins, *Law of Love*, pp. 99–116, 304–39.
15. Porter, *Moral Science*, p. 9. See also McCosh, *Scottish Philosophy*, pp. 152–53.
16. Mahan, *Moral Philosophy*, p. 34.
17. Wayland, *Moral Science*, pp. 150–73.
18. "Moral Philosophy," *Encyclopaedia Americana*, IX, 32.

Chapter 9

1. See Thomas Hobbes, *Human Nature* (London, 1651), Chapter IX, section 17; Hutcheson, *Inquiry*, Section II, article iii; and Butler's "Preface" to his *Fifteen Sermons Preached at Rolls Chapel*.
2. Hopkins, *Moral Science*, pp. 181–204.
3. See Reinhold Niebuhr, *An Interpretation of Christian Ethics* (New York, 1956; first published, 1935), pp. 43–62, 97–123.
4. See Robert Newton Flew, *Idea of Perfection in Christian Theology: An Historical Study of the Christian Ideal for the Present Life* (London, 1934), and Frederick Platt, "Perfection," in James Hastings, ed., *Encyclopaedia of Religion and Ethics* (New York, 1920), IX, 728–37.
5. Flew, *Idea of Perfection*, pp. 113–341; Platt, "Perfection," pp. 730–32.
6. On the dangers of identifying virtue and benevolence see Joseph Butler, "Nature of Virtue," *Analogy of Religion*, pp. 451–67. Mark Hopkins used the term "rational love" to refer to the rational ascertainment of and voluntary service to the highest well-being of God and the sentient universe. See his *Law of Love*, pp. 99–116. See also: Edwards, *True Virtue*, pp. 1–26; Finney, *Systematic Theology*, I, 209–213; Mahan, *Abstract*, 208–209; Dagg, *Moral Science*, pp. 79–80; Peabody, *Christian Morals*, pp. 147–48; James McCosh, *Our Moral Nature Being a Brief System of Ethics* (New York, 1892), pp. 8–11, 27–28. An exception was Archibald Alexander, who argued that virtue is *sui generis*, hence indefinable. See his *Moral Science*, pp. 141–208.

7. See Edwards, *True Virtue*, pp. 42–60, 85–97, and Samuel Hopkins, "An Inquiry into the Nature of True Holiness" (1773), *Works of Samuel Hopkins, D.D.* (three volumes; Boston, 1852), III, 23–30. On the emphasis on benevolence in early-nineteenth-century America see Perry Miller, *Life of the Mind in America from the Revolution to the Civil War* (New York, 1965), pp. 20 ff., 189–90.

8. Dagg, *Moral Science*, p. 25; Bowen, *Lowell Lectures*, pp. 297, 313.

9. Asa Mahan, *Scripture Doctrine of Christian Perfection* (Boston, 1839), pp. 9–10. A brief account of the Oberlin doctrine is offered by James Harris Fairchild, "The Decline of Sanctification at Oberlin," *Congregational Quarterly*, 8, ser. 2 (1876), 239–59. See also Walter E. C. Wright, "Oberlin's Contribution to Ethics," *Bibliotheca Sacra*, 57 (1900), 429–44, and Smith, *Revivalism and Social Reform*, pp. 103–13, where the Wesleyan roots of Oberlin perfectionism are noted.

10. Mahan, *Christian Perfection*, pp. 86–89.

11. George Peck, *Scripture Doctrine of Christian Perfection Stated and Defended* (New York, 1845), esp. pp. 47, 79, 97–99. For a detailed examination of Methodist thought in this period see Philip Wesley Ott, "The Mind of Early American Methodism: 1800–1844" (unpublished doctoral dissertation, University of Pennsylvania, 1968).

12. William Cochran, "Simplicity of Moral Actions," *Oberlin Evangelist*, 4 (1842), 33–35, 41–45.

13. On the difficulties created by Cochran's theory, see Fairchild, "Decline of Sanctification," *loc. cit.* For a discussion of the theory see Foster, *New England Theology*, pp. 458–64. From his own theological perspective, Finney had trouble reconciling the theory of the simplicity of moral actions with his conviction that perfection is to be achieved through a continual *growth* in grace.

14. Finney, *Systematic Theology*, I, 175.

15. *Ibid.*, II, 197–203.

16. *Ibid.*, I, 290–91. It is easy to see the similarity between this view and Edwards's idea of virtue.

17. *Ibid.*, I, 156, 158–73.

18. Rudolph Otto, *Idea of the Holy*, tr. John W. Harvey (New York, 1958; first published, 1923), pp. 12–24.

19. The implicit relativism of this view is evident in Mahan,

Christian Perfection, p. 9, and in Finney's lecture on sanctification in the *Oberlin Evangelist*, 2 (1840), 3.

20. James Harris Fairchild, *Moral Philosophy; Or, the Science of Obligation* (New York, 1869), p. 60. The more common custom is to distinguish between the imperative and the meritorious. See the article on "Moral Philosophy," *Encyclopaedia Americana* (1849 edition), IX, 32.

21. Mahan, *Moral Philosophy*, pp. 66–67.

22. Walker, *Sermons*, II, 143–47.

23. Charles C. Cole, Jr., *Social Theories of the Northern Evangelists* (New York, 1954), p. 189.

24. Alexander, *Moral Science*, pp. 255–58. See also Hopkins, *Law of Love*, pp. 99–116; and Adams, *Moral Philosophy*, p. 66.

25. On the "moral athleticism" of the New England Puritans see Ralph Barton Perry, *Puritanism and Democracy* (New York and Evanston, 1954; first published, 1944), pp. 245–68. On the Victorian concern with virtue see Houghton, *Victorian Frame of Mind*, pp. 228–42.

26. See William Ellery Channing, *The Perfect Life in Twelve Discourses*, William Henry Channing, ed. (1873); in the *Works of William Ellery Channing* (Boston, 1903), pp. 925–1020. On the idea of perfectibility from ancient times to the present, see John Passmore, *The Perfectibility of Man* (New York, 1970).

27. Walker, "Perfection and Christian Aim," *Sermons*, I, 450.

28. Wayland, *Moral Science*, p. 83.

29. Wayland, *Salvation by Christ*, pp. 37–38.

30. William James, "The Moral Philosopher and the Moral Life," *Will to Believe and Other Essays on Popular Philosophy* (New York and London, 1897), pp. 212–13.

31. See Staughton Lynd, *Intellectual Origins of American Radicalism* (New York, 1968), and Madden, *Civil Disobedience*, for two recent discussions of the radical implications of American social and ethical thought.

Chapter 10

1. Ralph Barton Perry, *General Theory of Value* (New York, 1926), pp. 5, 693.

2. Sometimes writers would use the term "natural law" to refer both to moral and physical laws. For a discussion of the subject see Benjamin F. Wright, Jr., *American Interpretations of Natural Law; A Study in the History of*

Political Thought (Cambridge, Massachusetts, 1931), esp. pp. 332–41.

3. Wayland, *Moral Science*, pp. 17–20; cf. pp. 103–104, 126–35. The three-fold meaning of "moral law" is discussed by Louise Saxe Eby, *The Quest for Moral Law* (New York, 1944), pp. 7–15.

4. Besides B. F. Wright, *op. cit.*, see Otto Gierke, *Natural Law and the Theory of Society, 1500–1800* (Boston, 1957; first published, 1934), with an introduction by the translator, Ernest Barker; and George Gurvitch, "Natural Law," *Encyclopaedia of the Social Sciences* (New York, 1937), XI, 284–90.

5. See Calvin's *Institutes*, Bk. II, Ch. VIII; Bk. III, Ch. XI.

6. Foster, *New England Theology*, pp. 113–17. Foster maintains that Bellamy was influenced both by Edwards and by Hugo Grotius in this matter.

7. *Ibid.*, pp. 113, 189–223, 510–11. See also Haroutunian, *Piety versus Moralism*, pp. 40–42.

8. Noah Porter, "Introduction" to Taylor, *Moral Government*, I, iii–viii. See also Foster, *New England Theology*, pp. 393–400.

9. Taylor, *Moral Government*, I, 7–17, 63–68; II, 265–73.

10. Robert Baird, *Religion in America*, p. 291.

11. Butler, *Analogy of Religion*, see Chapter III.

12. *Ibid.*, Chapter VII.

13. Alexander, *Moral Science*, pp. 209–10.

14. *Ibid.*, p. 254.

15. Finney, *Systematic Theology*, I, 4.

16. *Ibid.*, p. 6.

17. *Ibid.*, pp. 20–24; cf. pp. 176–87.

18. *Ibid.*, pp. 17–18.

19. On Taylor, see Mead, *Nathaniel William Taylor*, pp. 95–127. Finney's similarity to Taylor is discussed by Whitney R. Cross, *Burned-Over District: The Social and Intellectual History of Enthusiastic Religion in Western New York, 1800–1850* (Ithaca, New York, 1950), pp. 151–69.

20. Finney, *Systematic Theology*, I, 40.

21. Cross, *Burned-Over District*, p. 159. Peck, *Scripture Doctrine of Christian Perfection*, pp. 92–93 n., distinguished Finney's position from both the New Divinity and the Wesleyan doctrines.

22. See, for example, Hopkins, *Law of Love*, pp. 134, 143;

Porter, *Moral Science*, pp. 133–216; Mahan, *Abstract*, pp. 189–92, and *Moral Philosophy*, pp. 50–58; McCosh, *Divine Government*, *passim;* Alexander, *Moral Science*, pp. 253–55.

23. Bowen, *Lowell Lectures*, pp. 217–18.
24. *Ibid.*, pp. 67–111.
25. *Ibid.*, p. 92. For a somewhat similar point of view see Horace Bushnell, *Nature and the Supernatural, as Together Constituting One System of God* (New York, 1858), esp. pp. 250–75.
26. Bowen, *Lowell Lectures*, p. 283; see pp. 282–87.
27. Josiah Royce, *Religious Aspect of Philosophy* (New York, 1885), p. 219.
28. Mahan, *Moral Philosophy*, p. 273.

Chapter 11

1. Mahan, *Abstract*, p. 25. See also McCosh, *Divine Government*, pp. 227–61.
2. Eliphalet Nott, *Counsels to Young Men of the Formation of Character, and the Principles which Lead to Success and Happiness in Life* (New York, 1840), pp. 35–36; Wayland, *Moral Science*, p. 93. See also Dagg, *Moral Science*, pp. 43, 63.
3. See Hopkins, *Moral Science*, pp. 93–95; and Wayland, *Moral Science*, pp. 94–99.
4. McCosh, *Our Moral Nature*, p. 19.
5. For a discussion of this process of secularization with reference to Henry Ward Beecher, see Clifford E. Clark, Jr., "The Changing Nature of Protestantism in Mid-Nineteenth Century America: Henry Ward Beecher's *Seven Lectures to Young Men*," *Journal of American History*, 57 (1971), 832–46.
6. Francis Wayland, *Elements of Political Economy* (Boston, 1852; first published, 1837), pp. 383–87.
7. Dietrich Bonhoeffer, *Prisoner for God* (New York, 1959), p. 123. For further elaboration see also Harvey Cox, *The Secular City* (New York, 1965), Chapter 11.
8. Bowen, *Political Economy*, p. 27.
9. Henry Vethake, *Principles of Political Economy* (Philadelphia, 1838), pp. 405–6; see also p. 310.
10. Alonzo Potter, *Political Economy: Its Objects, Uses, and Principles* (New York, 1840), pp. 84, 86; see pp. 17–19, 81–86.

11. Bowen, *Political Economy*, p. 27; see also pp. 18–19.
12. Francis Wayland, *Occasional Discourses* (Boston, 1833), p. 146.
13. See Bryson, *Man and Society*, pp. 173–238.
14. Wayland, *Political Economy*, p. iv.
15. Bowen, *Political Economy*, p. 17.
16. *Ibid.*, pp. 76–82.
17. Wayland, *Political Economy*, p. 131.
18. This kind of moralistic interpretation of economic principles was common at the time. For further discussion of economic and ethical thinking in nineteenth-century America, see: Charles H. Hopkins, *Rise of the Social Gospel in American Protestantism, 1865–1915* (New Haven, 1940); Michael J. L. O'Connor, *Origins of Academic Economics in the United States* (New York, 1944); Henry F. May, *Protestant Churches and Industrial America* (New York, 1949); Joseph Dorfman, *The Economic Mind in American Civilization, 1606–1865* (two volumes; New York, 1954; first published, 1946), II; and Sidney Fine, *Laissez-Faire and the General Welfare State: A Study of Conflict in American Thought, 1865–1901* (Ann Arbor, 1956).
19. John McVickar, "Concluding Remarks," in his republication of J. R. McCulloch's *Outlines of Political Economy* (New York, 1825), pp. 136–37; cf. p. 69 n.
20. Bowen, *Political Economy*, p. 19. See also Mark Hopkins, *The Law of Progress: A Centennial Discourse, before the Alumni of Williams College* (North Adams, Massachusetts, 1876).
21. On millennial thought see Ernest L. Tuveson, *Redeemer Nation: The Idea of America's Millennial Role* (Chicago and London, 1968). My observations on the idea of culture are based on my reading of the educational theories of the academic moralists and on allusions to culture in the treatises on political economy. John Higham, in offering "Some Reflections on the 1850s," a lecture delivered at the University of California, Berkeley, February 24, 1966, has suggested that the mid-nineteenth-century concern with "civilization" signaled a transition from evangelicalism to gentility, and also reflected a new class consciousness. Higham's arguments seem plausible.
22. Henry F. May, *The End of American Innocence: The First Years of Our Own Time, 1912–1917* (New York, 1959), pp. 9–19. On the change in evangelical religion

see McLoughlin, *The Meaning of Henry Ward Beecher.*

23. For a recent, instructive discussion of the genteel tradition see John Tomsich, *A Genteel Endeavor: American Culture and Politics in the Gilded Age* (Stanford, California, 1971).

Chapter 12

1. Ferdinand Tönnies, *Community and Society*, tr. Charles P. Loomis (East Lansing, Michigan, 1957; first German edition, 1887), pp. 33–34.
2. Benjamin Franklin offered a similar maxim: "Resolve to perform what you ought; perform without fail what you resolve."
3. Smith, *Professors and Public Ethics*, pp. 77–80. See also Howe, *The Unitarian Conscience*, pp. 205–35.
4. As an example of this quality of life see Charles G. Sellers, Jr., *James K. Polk: Jacksonian, 1795–1843* (Princeton, 1957), pp. viii–ix, 3–32. See also Marvin Meyers, *The Jacksonian Persuasion: Politics and Belief* (Palo Alto, California, 1957).
5. Hopkins, *Moral Science*, pp. 95–96. See also Dagg, *Moral Science*, pp. 234–38.
6. John Locke, *Second Treatise of Civil Government* (1690); in T. J. Cook, ed., *Locke's Two Treatises of Government* (New York, 1947), p. 159.
7. *Ibid.*, pp. 168–69. For a historical treatment of the assumptions and attitudes that lay behind Locke's treatises, see John Dunn, *The Political Thought of John Locke* (Oxford, 1969).
8. Hopkins, *Law of Love*, pp. 268–69.
9. McCosh, *Our Moral Nature*, p. 47.
10. The Harvard moral philosophers, for example, rejected the contract theory of the state, preferring the Burkean view that social institutions are of divine rather than human origin. See Howe, *Unitarian Conscience*, pp. 121–31.
11. Haven, *Moral Philosophy*, pp. 228–29. Wayland took a somewhat similar position in his *Moral Science*, esp. pp. 311–16.
12. For a recent defence of the social-contract theory as an interpretation of political obligation see Joseph Tussmann, *Obligation and the Body Politic* (New York, 1960).
13. Hopkins, *Law of Love*, p. 270. On the effect of the Civil

War on social theories of Northern intellectuals, see George M. Fredrickson, *The Inner Civil War: Northern Intellectuals and the Crisis of the Union* (New York, 1965).

14. Finney, *Systematic Theology*, I, 425–35; Wayland, *Salvation by Christ*, p. 357.

15. Paul Tillich, *Theology and Culture*, Robert Kimball, ed. (New York, 1964), esp. pp. 133–38. See also his *Morality and Beyond* (New York, 1963), pp. 17–30.

16. Wayland, *Moral Science*, p. 327; cf. Finney, *Systematic Theology*, pp. 437–39.

17. On the political involvements of the academic philosophers, see Smith, *Professors and Public Ethics*.

18. Philip Lindsley, *Works of Philip Lindsley, D.D.* (three volumes; Philadelphia and Nashville, 1859), I, 235. See also Thomas C. Upham, *Life of Faith* (Boston, 1845), pp. 296–99.

19. On the mugwump mentality see John G. Sproat, *"The Best Men": Liberal Reformers in the Gilded Age* (New York, 1968); Robert L. Beisner, *Twelve against Empire: The Anti-Imperialists, 1898–1900* (New York, 1968), pp. 5–17; and Geoffrey Blodgett, "Reform Thought and the Genteel Tradition," *The Gilded Age*, H. W. Morgan, ed. (revised edition; Syracuse, New York, 1970), pp. 55–76.

20. Wayland, *Human Responsibility*, pp. 90–120; cf. Asa Mahan, "Reform," *Oberlin Evangelist*, 6 (1844), 9.

21. Upham, *Life of Faith*, p. 298.

22. Wayland, *Human Responsibility*, *passim*.

23. On the place of academic moral philosophy in the slavery debate see Smith, *Professors and Public Ethics*, esp. pp. 67–70. See also Howe, *Unitarian Conscience*, pp. 270–305.

24. Haven, *Moral Philosophy*, pp. 276–77. See also Wayland, *Moral Science*, pp. 336–38; Adams, *Moral Philosophy*, pp. 100–102; Finney, *Systematic Theology*, I, 439–40. The subject is discussed in detail by Madden, *Civil Disobedience*, pp. 30–43, 70–84.

25. Adams, *Moral Philosophy*, pp. 101, 102.

26. See Wayland's *Human Responsibility*, pp. 161–88, for his treatment of slavery.

27. Wayland's point of view is treated sympathetically by Edward H. Madden, "Francis Wayland and the Limits of

Moral Responsibility," American Philosophical Society, *Proceedings*, 106 (1962), 352–58.

28. See Walter Lippmann, *Essays in the Public Philosophy* (Boston, 1955), esp. Chapter 8.

29. See Daniel Aaron, *Men of Good Hope: A Story of American Progressives* (New York, 1961), esp. Part II, pp. 55–242.

30. William Henry Seward, speech in the United States Senate, March 11, 1850, *Congressional Globe*, 31st Congress, 2nd session, appendix, pp. 262–76.

Chapter 13

1. Andover Seminary, *Memorial of the Semi-Centennial Celebration of the Founding of the Theological Seminary at Andover* (Andover, 1859), pp. 156–69. See also Wayland, *Memoir*, I, 60–61.

2. Davis, *The Half-Century*, p. 222.

3. *Ibid.*, Hopkins's Introduction, esp. pp. xiii–xxiii.

4. See, for example, Denison, *Mark Hopkins*, pp. 241–42.

5. Schneider, *History of American Philosophy*, p. 226.

6. See Schmidt, *Old Time College President*, pp. 139–43.

7. Smith, *Professors and Public Ethics*, pp. 211–214, lists the various social concerns of the academic moralists.

8. At Harvard, for example, prospective ministers were taught how to guide the moral behavior of their communities by policing libraries, working on school boards, and watching over recreational diversions. See Howe, *Unitarian Conscience*, pp. 131–37. On the impact of the lyceum in antebellum America see Carl Bode, *The American Lyceum: Town Meeting of the Mind* (New York, 1956), esp. pp. 36, 124–25, 213–14.

9. Except for Wayland and a few others, the moral philosophy textbook writers usually gave only perfunctory attention to the slavery question, and frequently did not deal with it at all.

10. Wayland, "The Perils of Riches," *Sermons to the Churches*, esp. pp. 218–27.

11. Wayland, "Slavery to Public Opinion," *ibid.*, p. 193.

12. Wayland, "A Consistent Piety, the Demand of the Age," *ibid.*, pp. 153–58. On the increasing conservatism and secularity of American society in the mid-nineteenth century see John Higham, *From Boundlessness to Consolidation:*

The Transformation of American Culture, 1848–1860 (Ann Arbor, 1969).

13. Wayland, letter to J. W. Alexander (1854), *Memoir*, II, 177.
14. Walker, Sermon on "Providence," *Sermons*, I, 62–63. The same concern is evident throughout Bowen's *Lowell Lectures*.
15. Bushnell, *Nature and the Supernatural*, pp. 13–35.
16. C. S. Lewis, *De Descriptione Temporum* (Cambridge, England, 1955), pp. 10–11. On the impact of evolutional thinking see: John Dewey, *The Influence of Darwinism on Philosophy* (New York, 1910), pp. 1–19; John C. Greene, *The Death of Adam: Evolution and Its Impact on Western Thought* (Ames, Iowa, 1959); and Gertrude Himmelfarb, *Darwin and the Darwinian Revolution* (New York, 1968; first published, 1959).
17. John Bascom, *Ethics, or Science of Duty* (New York, 1879), esp. pp. 354–78; quotation, p. 354.
18. See G. Stanley Hall, "The Philosophy of the Future," *Nation*, 27 (1878), 283–84.
19. Richard Hofstadter, *Social Darwinism in American Thought* (revised edition; Boston, 1955), pp. 31–50.
20. Schneider, *History of American Philosophy*, pp. 241–42, 441–54.
21. See Edward A. Ross, *Sin and Society: An Analysis of Latter-Day Iniquity* (Boston, 1907), on the effect of corporate industrialism on the old morality. For a recent analysis, see Robert H. Wiebe, *The Search for Order, 1877–1920* (New York, 1967), pp. 11–75, 133–63.
22. Veysey, *Emergence of the American University*, pp. 21–56. See also George F. Peterson, *The New England College in the Age of the University* (Amherst, Massachusetts, 1964).
23. See Gladys Bryson, "The Emergence of the Social Sciences from Moral Philosophy," *International Journal of Ethics*, 42 (1932), 304–23.
24. James, *Will to Believe*, pp. 202–203.

Chapter 14

1. Wayland, *Moral Science*, preface to the second edition, pp. 6–7. On the necessity of formal recitation to ensure the

student's "fidelity" to his studies, see also Noah Porter, *The American Colleges and the American Public* (New Haven, 1870), pp. 134–47.

2. In Wayland, *Memoir*, I, 245–48.

3. *The Education of Henry Adams* (New York, 1931; first published, 1918), p. 55. Cf. George Santayana, *Character and Opinion in the United States* (New York, 1920), Chapter II. An excellent account of the often lively social and intellectual life of an alert student in the old-time college is William Gardiner Hammond, *Remembrance of Amherst: An Undergraduate Diary, 1846–1848*, George F. Whicher, ed. (New York, 1956).

4. Schneider, *History of American Philosophy*, pp. 225–26.

5. McCosh, *Divine Government*, p. 3. Wayland, *Memoir*, I, 232. See also Mark Hopkins, *Moral Science*, pp. ix–x.

6. Perry Miller describes the Scottish philosophy of common sense as "the official metaphysic of America" from the 1820's through the 1870's. I think it more accurate to apply this appellation to the more comprehensive system of ideas represented in the textbooks on mental and moral philosophy. See Miller's Introduction to his *American Thought from the Civil War to World War I* (New York, 1962), p. ix.

7. On this see Higham, *From Boundlessness to Consolidation*.

8. John R. Bodo, *The Protestant Clergy and Public Issues, 1812–1848* (Princeton, 1954), p. 156 n., correctly observes that Wayland gave philosophical voice to Protestant evangelicalism. See also William G. McLoughlin, ed., *The American Evangelicals, 1800–1900* (New York, 1968), pp. 3–4.

9. Miller, *Life of the Mind in America*, p. 318.

10. William Kingdon Clifford, "Cosmic Emotion" (1877), in his *Lectures and Essays*, Leslie Stephen and Frederick Pollock, ed. (two volumes; London, 1879), II, 253–83. The term was first introduced by Henry Sidgwick.

11. For a perceptive discussion of the Victorian ethic in Britain, see Trygve R. Tholfsen, "Intellectual Origins of Mid-Victorian Stability," *Political Science Quarterly*, 86 (1971), 57–91. See also Gertrude Himmelfarb, *Victorian Minds: A Study of Intellectuals in Crisis and of Ideologies in Transition* (New York, Evanston, London, 1968), pp. 279–99.

12. Walter Lippmann, *Public Opinion* (New York, 1960; first published, 1922), p. 122.
13. Vethake, *Political Economy*, p. 310.
14. Francis Wayland, *Occasional Discourses, Including Several Never before Published* (Boston, 1833), pp. 59–79.
15. Schaff, *America*, p. 43.
16. G. Stanley Hall, "Philosophy in the United States," *loc. cit.*, pp. 93–94.
17. *Ibid.*, p. 94.
18. Walt Whitman, *Democratic Vistas* (1871); in John Kouwenhoven, ed., *Leaves of Grass and Selected Prose* (New York, 1950), p. 463.
19. Van Wyck Brooks, *America's Coming of Age* (New York, 1958; first published, 1916), pp. 3, 9–10. A similar observation had been made earlier by George Santayana in his classic address "The Genteel Tradition in American Philosophy," 1911.
20. Walker, *Sermons*, II, 138.
21. Letter to Mrs. William L. Stone (n.d.) in Wayland, *Memoir*, I, 136–37.
22. *Ibid.*, p. 381.

Bibliography

Primary Materials

Adams, Jasper. *Elements of Moral Philosophy*. Philadelphia, 1837.

Alexander, Archibald. *Outlines of Moral Science*. New York, 1852.

———. Review of Francis Wayland's *Elements of Moral Science*. In [*The Princeton Review and*] *Biblical Repository*. Ser. 2nd, 7 (1835), 377–400.

Bain, Alexander. *Mental and Moral Science: A Compendium of Psychology and Ethics*. London, 1868.

Baird, Robert. *Religion in America*. New York, 1844.

Bascom, John. *Ethics or Science of Duty*. New York, 1879.

Beattie, James. *An Essay on the Nature and Immutability of Truth, in Opposition to Sophistry and Skepticism*. Sixth edition; Edinburgh, 1805; first published, 1770.

Beecher, Lyman. *Autobiography of Lyman Beecher*. Barbara M. Cross, ed. Cambridge, Massachusetts, 1961; first edition, 1864.

———. *Works*. Three volumes. Boston and Cleveland, 1852.

Bigelow, Jacob. *Elements of Technology*. Boston, 1829.

Bowen, Francis. *Critical Essays on a Few Subjects Connected with the History and Present Condition of Speculative Philosophy*. Boston, 1842.

———. *Lowell Lectures, on the Application of Metaphysical and Ethical Science to the Evidences of Religion*. Boston, 1849.

Bowen, Francis. *Principles of Political Economy Applied to the Condition, the Resources, and the Institutions of the American People.* Boston, 1856.

———. Review of Francis Wayland's *Elements of Moral Science.* In *The Christian Examiner and General Review,* 22 (1837), 364–82.

Brown, Thomas. *Lectures on Ethics.* Edinburgh, 1846.

Buck, Charles. *A Theological Dictionary, Containing Definitions of all Religious Terms.* Philadelphia, 1825.

Burton, Asa. *Essays on Some of the First Principles of Meta-Physicks, Ethicks, and Theology.* Portland, Maine, 1824.

Bushnell, Horace. *Christian Nurture.* New Haven, 1947; first published, 1861.

———. *Nature and the Supernatural, as Together Constituting One System of God.* New York, 1858.

———. *Politics Under the Law of God.* Hartford, 1844.

Butler, Joseph. *The Analogy of Religion, Natural and Revealed, to the Constitution and Course of Nature, to Which are Added Two brief Dissertations: I. Of Personal Identity. II. Of the Nature of Virtue.* Fourth edition. London, 1750. First published, 1736.

———. *Fifteen Sermons Preached at the Rolls Chapel.* London, 1726.

Channing, William Ellery. *The Works of William Ellery Channing, D.D.* Boston, 1903.

Clap, Thomas. *An Essay on the Nature and Foundation of Moral Virtue and Obligation; Being a Short Introduction to the Study of Ethics; For the Use of the Students of Yale-College.* New Haven, 1765.

Cochran, William. "Simplicity of Moral Actions," *Oberlin Evangelist,* 4 (1842), 33–35, 41–45.

[Colton, Calvin.] *Protestant Jesuitism.* New York, 1836.

Colton, Calvin. *Thoughts on the Religious State of the Country* [the United States]; *With Reasons for Preferring the Episcopacy.* London, 1837.

Cousin, Victor. *Lectures on the True, the Beautiful, and the Good.* O. W. Wright, tr. New York, 1854.

Cudworth, Ralph. *A Treatise Concerning Eternal and Immutable Morality.* London, 1731.

Dagg, John Leadley. *The Elements of Moral Science.* New York, 1859.

Davis, Emerson. *The Half-Century or, a History of the Changes That Have Transpired, Chiefly in the United States, between*

1800 and 1850. With an Introduction by Mark Hopkins. Boston, 1851.

Day, Jeremiah. *An Examination of President Edwards's Inquiry on the Freedom of the Will*. New Haven, 1841.

Doddridge, Philip. *A Course of Lectures on the Principal Subjects in Pneumatology, Ethics, and Divinity; With References to the Most Considerable Authors on Each Subject*. Two volumes. Third edition. London, 1794. First edition, 1763.

Dwight, Timothy. *Theology Explained and Defended in a Series of Sermons*. Four volumes. New York, 1849. First published, 1818.

Dymond, Jonathan. *Essays on the Principles of Morality, and on the Private and Political Rights and Obligations of Mankind*. New York, 1845.

Edwards, Jonathan. *A Careful and Strict Enquiry into the Modern Prevailing Notions of that Freedom of Will, Which is Supposed to be Essential to Moral Agency, Vertue and Vice, Reward and Punishment, Praise and Blame*. Paul Ramsey, ed. New Haven, 1957; first published, 1754.

———. *The Nature of True Virtue*. William K. Frankena, ed. Ann Arbor, Michigan, 1960; first published, 1765.

Emerson, Ralph Waldo. "The Present State of Ethical Philosophy" (1821). In Kenneth Walter Cameron, ed., *Transcendental Climate: New Resources for the Study of Emerson, Thoreau, and Their Contemporaries*. Three volumes. Hartford, 1963. I, 11–20.

Everett, Edward. *Orations and Speeches on Various Occasions*. Boston, 1853.

Fairchild, James H. "The Decline of Sanctification at Oberlin," *Congregational Quarterly*, 18 (1876), 239–59.

———. *Moral Philosophy; or the Science of Obligation*. New York, 1869.

Finney, Charles Grandison. *Lectures on Revivals of Religion*. William G. McLoughlin, ed. Cambridge, Massachusetts, 1960; first published, 1835.

———. *Lectures on Systematic Theology*. Two volumes. Oberlin, 1846, 1847.

Gros, John Daniel. *Natural Principles of Rectitude for the Conduct of Man in All States and Situations of Life Demonstrated and Explained in a Systematic Treatise on Moral Philosophy Comprehending the Law of Nature—Ethics—Natural Juris-*

prudence—General Economics—Politics—and the Law of Nations. New York, 1795.

Grund, Francis J. *The Americans in Their Moral, Social, and Political Relations.* Two volumes. London, 1837.

Hamilton, William. *Lectures on Metaphysics and Logic.* H. L. Mansel and John Veitch, ed. Four volumes. Edinburgh, London, Boston, 1859–60.

Hammond, William Gardiner. *Remembrance of Amherst; An Undergraduate Diary, 1846–1848.* George F. Whicher, ed. New York, 1956.

Haven, Joseph. *Moral Philosophy: Including Theoretical and Practical Ethics.* New York, 1859.

Henry, Caleb Sprague. *Considerations on Some of the Elements and Conditions of Social Welfare and Human Progress. Being Academic and Occasional Discourses and Other Pieces.* New York, 1861.

Hickok, Laurens Perseus. *Rational Psychology; or, the Subjective Idea and Objective Law of All Intelligence.* Boston, 1861.

———. *A System of Moral Science.* Schenectady, New York, 1853. Revised, with cooperation of Julius H. Seelye: Boston, 1880.

Hildreth, Richard. "A Joint Letter to Orestes A. Brownson and the Editor of the 'North American Review' [Francis Bowen]: In which the Editor of the North American Review Is Proved to Be No Christian and Little Better Than an Atheist." In *An American Utilitarian: Richard Hildreth as a Philosopher,* Martha M. Pingel, ed. New York, 1948, pp. 153–76.

———. *Theory of Morals: An Inquiry Concerning the Law of Moral Distinctions and the Variations and Contradictions of Ethical Codes.* Boston, 1844.

Hopkins, Mark. *The Law of Love and Love as a Law; Or, Moral Science, Theoretical and Practical.* New York, 1869.

———. *Lectures on the Evidence of Christiantity.* Boston, 1846.

———. *Lectures on Moral Science.* Boston, 1862.

Hopkins, Samuel. *An Inquiry into the Nature of True Holiness* (1773). In *The Works of Samuel Hopkins, D.D.* Three volumes. Boston, 1852. III.

Hume, David. *Essays, Moral, Political, and Literary.* Two volumes. London, 1882. First published, 1741, 1742.

———. *An Inquiry Concerning the Principles of Morals.* Charles W. Hendel, ed. New York, 1957. First published, 1751.

Hume, David. *A Treatise of Human Nature.* L. A. Selby-Bigge, ed. Oxford, 1888. First published, 1739–40.

Hutcheson, Francis. *Inquiry into the Original of Our Ideas of Beauty and Virtue.* London, 1725.

———. *Essay on the Nature and Conduct of the Passions with Illustrations from the Moral Sense.* London, 1738.

Johnson, Samuel. *Elementa Philosophica: Containing Chiefly, Noetica, or Things Relating to the Mind or Understanding; and Ethica, or Things Relating to Moral Behavior.* Philadelphia, 1752.

Jouffroy, Theodore. *Introduction to Ethics, Including a Critical Survey of Moral Systems.* William H. Channing, tr. Two volumes. Boston, 1840.

Kant, Immanuel. *The Doctrine of Virtue.* Mary J. Gregor, tr. New York, Evanston, London, 1964. First German edition, 1797.

———. *Foundations of the Metaphysics of Morals.* Lewis White Beck, tr. Indianapolis and New York, 1959. First German edition, 1785.

———. *Lectures on Ethics.* Louis Infield, tr. New York and Evanston, 1963; 1930. Originally delivered in 1775–80.

Lieber, Francis (ed.) *Encyclopaedia Americana.* Revised edition. Philadelphia, 1849. First edition, 1831.

———. *Manual of Political Ethics Designed Chiefly for the Use of Colleges and Students at Law.* Two volumes. Boston, 1838, 1839.

———. *The Miscellaneous Writings of Francis Lieber.* Two volumes. Philadelphia, 1881.

Lindsley, Philip. *The Works of Philip Lindsley, D.D.* Two volumes. Philadelphia and Nashville, 1859.

Locke, John. *An Essay Concerning Human Understanding.* Alexander Campbell Fraser, ed. Two volumes. New York, 1959. Locke's *Essay* first appeared in 1690.

McCosh, James. *The Method of Divine Government Physical and Moral.* Twelfth edition. London, 1883. First edition, 1850.

———. *Our Moral Nature Being a Brief System of Ethics.* New York, 1892.

———. *Philosophy of Reality: Should It Be Favored by America?* New York, 1894.

———. *Psychology: The Cognitive Powers.* New York, 1886.

197

McCosh, James. *Psychology: the Motive Powers, Emotion, Conscience, Will.* New York, 1887.

―――. *The Scottish Philosophy, Biographical, Expository, Critical, from Hutcheson to Hamilton.* New York, 1875.

Mackintosh, James. *A General View of the Progress of Ethical Philosophy, Chiefly during the Seventeenth and Eighteenth Centuries.* London, 1832.

McVickar, John. *Outlines of Political Economy: Being a Republication of the Article upon that Subject* [by J. R. McCulloch] *Contained in the Edinburgh Supplement to the Encyclopaedia Britannica. Together with Notes Explanatory and Critical, and a Summary of the Science.* New York, 1825.

Mahan, Asa. *Abstract of a Course of Lectures on Mental and Moral Philosophy.* Oberlin, 1840.

―――. *Autobiography: Intellectual, Moral, and Spiritual.* London, 1882.

―――. *Out of Darkness into Light.* London, 1877.

―――. "Reform," *Oberlin Evangelist,* 6 (1844), 45, 51–52, 67, 76, 99, 121, 130–31.

―――. *Science of Moral Philosophy.* Oberlin, 1848.

―――. *Scripture Doctrine of Christian Perfection.* Boston, 1839.

Mann, Horace. *Lectures on Education.* Boston, 1850.

Marsh, James. *The Remains of the Rev. James Marsh, D.D.* Burlington, Vermont, 1843.

Merriam, George S. (ed.). *Noah Porter: A Memorial by Friends.* New York, 1893.

Mill, John Stuart. *Mill's Ethical Writings.* J. B. Schneewind, ed. New York, 1965.

Miller, Samuel. *A Brief Retrospect of the Eightenth Cenutry.* Two volumes. New York, 1803.

Nichols, Thomas Low. *Forty Years of American Life.* London, 1864.

Nott, Eliphalet. *Counsels to Young Men on the Formation of Character, and the Principles Which Lead to Success and Happiness in Life.* New York, 1840.

―――. *Miscellaneous Works.* Schenectady, New York, 1810.

Olin, Stephen. *The Works of Stephen Olin, D.D., LL.D.* Two volumes. New York, 1852.

Paley, William. *The Principles of Moral and Political Philosophy* (1785). In *The Works of William Paley, D.D.* Philadelphia, 1831, pp. 21–165.

Park, Edwards Amassa. *The Theology of the Intellect and That of the Feelings.* Boston, 1850.

Peabody, Andrew Preston. *Christian Morals; A Series of Lectures.* Boston, 1887.

———. *A Manual of Moral Philosophy.* New York, 1873.

Peck, George. *The Scripture Doctrine of Christian Perfection Stated and Defended.* Abridged edition; New York, 1845.

Porter, Noah. *The American Colleges and the American Public.* New York, 1878.

———. *Elements of Moral Science, Theoretical and Practical.* New York, 1884.

———. "On Moral Science, as a Branch of Academical Education," *Quarterly Christian Spectator,* ser. 3rd, 6 (1834), 561–80.

———. *The Sciences of Nature versus the Science of Man; A Plea for the Science of Man.* New York, 1871.

Potter, Alonzo. *Political Economy: Its Objects, Uses, and Principles: Considered with Reference to the Condition of the American People.* New York, 1840.

Price, Richard. *A Review of the Principal Questions in Morals.* D. Daiches Raphael, ed. London, 1948; from the twelfth edition, 1787. First published, 1758.

Reid, Thomas. *Essays on the Active Powers of Man* (1788). Volume II of *The Works of Thomas Reid, D.D.* Sir William Hamilton, ed. Two volumes. Edinburgh, 1863.

———. *An Inquiry into the Human Mind, on the Principles of Common Sense.* Second edition, corrected. Edinburgh and London, 1765. First edition, 1764.

Rush, Benjamin. *An Inquiry into the Influence of Physical Causes upon the Moral Faculty.* Philadelphia, 1789.

Schaff, Philip. *America. A Sketch of the Political, Social, and Religious Character of the United States of North America.* New York, 1855.

Selby-Bigge, L. A. (ed.) *British Moralists; Being Selections from Writers Principally of the Eighteenth Century.* Two volumes. Oxford, 1897.

Shaftesbury, Third Earl of (Anthony Ashley Cooper). *Characteristics of Men, Manners, Opinions, Times.* London, 1711.

Sidgwick, Henry. *The Methods of Ethics.* Chicago, 1962; seventh edition, 1907. First edition, 1874.

Smith, Samuel Stanhope. *The Lectures, Corrected and Improved, Which Have Been Delivered for a Series of Years, in the College of New Jersey; On the Subjects of Moral and Political Philosophy.* Two Volumes. Trenton, New Jersey, 1812.

Smith, William Andrew. *Lectures on the Philosophy and Practice of Slavery, as Exhibited in the Institution of Domestic Slavery in the United States: With the Duties of Masters to Slaves.* Nashville, 1856.

Spencer, Herbert. *The Data of Ethics.* Third edition. London, 1881.

————. *The Principles of Ethics.* Two volumes. New York, 1897. First published, 1892, 1893.

Stewart, Dugald. *The Philosophy of the Active and Moral Powers of Man* (1828). Volumes VI and VII of *The Collected Works of Dugald Stewart, Esq., F.R.S.S.* Sir William Hamilton, ed. Edinburgh and Boston, 1855.

Stowe, Harriet Beecher. *Oldtown Folks.* Henry F. May, ed. Cambridge, Massachusetts, 1966; first edition, 1869.

Tappan, Henry Phillip. *A Review of Edwards's "Inquiry into the Freedom of the Will."* New York, 1839.

Taylor, Nathaniel William. *Lectures on the Moral Government of God.* Two volumes. New York, 1859.

Upham, Thomas Cogswell. *Elements of Intellectual Philosophy, Designed as a Text-Book.* Portland, Maine, 1827.

————. *The Life of Faith.* Boston, 1845.

Vethake, Henry. *Principles of Political Economy.* Philadelphia, 1838.

Walker, James. *Sermons Preached Chiefly in the College Chapel.* Two volumes. Boston, 1892.

Wayland, Francis. *Elements of Intellectual Philosophy.* Revised edition. New York, 1865. First edition, 1854.

————. *Elements of Moral Science.* Joseph L. Blau, ed. Cambridge, Massachusetts, 1963. First published, 1835; revised, 1865.

————. *Elements of Political Economy.* Boston, 1837.

————. *Limitations of Human Responsibility.* Boston, 1838.

————. "Moral Characteristics of the Nineteenth Century," *Quarterly Christian Spectator,* 5 (1833), 193–207.

————. *Occasional Discourses, Including Several Never before Published.* Boston, 1833.

————. *Report to the Corporation of Brown University, on Changes in the System of Collegiate Instruction.* Providence, 1850.

Wayland, Francis. *Salvation by Christ*. Boston, 1859.

———. *Sermons to the Churches*. Boston and London, 1858.

———. *Thoughts on the Present Collegiate System in the United States*. Boston, 1842.

Wayland, Francis (Jr.) and H. L. *A Memoir of the Life and Labors of Francis Wayland, D.D., LL.D*. Two volumes. New York, 1867.

Whewell, William. *Elements of Morality, Including Polity*. Two volumes. London, 1845.

———. *Lectures on the History of Moral Philosophy in England*. London, 1852.

Witherspoon, John. *Lectures on Moral Philosophy*. Princeton, 1912; first published, 1800.

Woods, Leonard. *An Examination of the Doctrine of Perfection, as Held by Rev. Asa Mahan, President of the Oberlin Collegiate Institute, Ohio, and Others*. New York, 1842.

Selected Secondary Works

Aaron, Daniel. *Men of Good Hope: A Story of American Progressives*. New York, 1951.

Ahlstrom, Sydney. "The Scottish Philosophy and American Theology," *Church History*, 24 (1955), 257–72.

Anderson, Quentin. *The Imperial Self: An Essay in American Literary and Cultural History*. New York, 1971.

Appelman, Philip; Madden, William; Wolff, Michael (ed.). *1859: Entering an Age of Crisis*. Bloomington, Indiana, 1959.

Arendt, Hannah. "Reflections: Civil Disobedience," *New Yorker* (September 12, 1970), 70–105.

Baker, Herschel. *The Image of Man: A Study of the Idea of Human Dignity in Classical Antiquity, the Middle Ages, and the Renaissance*. New York, 1947.

Barnes, Gilbert Hobbs. *The Anti-Slavery Impulse, 1830–1844*. New York, 1963; first published, 1933.

Barlow, Mark. "An Analysis of Moral Philosophy and Its Decline in Nineteenth Century American Colleges." Unpublished doctoral dissertation, Cornell University, 1962.

Bellah, Robert N. *Beyond Belief: Essays on Religion in a Post-Traditional World*. New York, Evanston, London, 1970.

Billington, Ray Allen. *The Protestant Crusade, 1800–1860; A Study of the Origins of American Nativism*. New York, 1938.

Blau, Joseph L. *Men and Movements in American Philosophy.* New York, 1952.

Blodgett, Geoffrey, "Reform Thought and the Genteel Tradition," *The Gilded Age,* H. Wayne Morgan, ed. Revised and enlarged edition. Syracuse, New York, 1970, pp. 55–76.

Bodo, John R. *The Protestant Clergy and Public Issues, 1812–1848.* Princeton, New Jersey, 1954.

Bonar, James. *The Moral Sense.* New York and London, 1930.

Branch, E. Douglas. *The Sentimental Years, 1836–1860.* New York, 1934.

Brennan, Bernard P. *The Ethics of William James.* New Haven, 1961.

Broad, C. D. *Five Types of Ethical Theory.* London, 1930.

Brooks, Van Wyck. *The Flowering of New England, 1815–1865.* New York, 1936.

———. *New England: Indian Summer.* New York, 1940.

———. *Three Essays on America.* New York, 1934.

Brown, Bernard E. *American Conservatives: The Political Thought of Francis Lieber and John Burgess.* New York, 1951.

Brunner, Emil. *The Divine Imperative: A Study in Christian Ethics.* Olive Wyon, tr. Philadelphia, 1947. First German edition, 1932.

Bryson, Gladys. "The Comparable Interests of the Old Moral Philosophy and the Modern Social Sciences," *Social Forces,* 11 (1932), 19–27.

———. "The Emergence of the Social Sciences from Moral Philosophy," *International Journal of Ethics,* 42 (1932), 304–23.

———. *Man and Society: The Scottish Inquiry of the Eighteenth Century.* Princeton, 1945.

———. "Sociology Considered as Moral Philosophy," *Sociological Review,* 24 (1932), 26–36.

Burn, W. L. *The Age of Equipoise: A Study of the Mid-Victorian Generation.* London, 1964.

Burns, Edward M. *The American Idea of Mission: Concepts of National Purpose and Destiny.* New Brunswick, New Jersey. 1957.

Butts, R. Freeman. *The College Charts Its Course: Historical Conceptions and Current Proposals.* New York and London, 1939.

———. *The American Tradition in Religion and Education.* Boston, 1950.

Castle, E. B. *Educating the Good Man: Moral Education in Christian Times.* New York, 1962. First published, 1958.

Clebsch, William A. *From Sacred to Profane America: The Role of Religion in American History.* New York, 1968.

Cole, Charles C., Jr. *The Social Ideas of the Northern Evangelists, 1826–1860.* New York, 1954.

Cragg, Gerald R. *Reason and Authority in the Eighteenth Century.* Cambridge, England, 1964.

Crocker, Lester G. *An Age of Crisis: Man and World in Eighteenth Century French Thought.* Baltimore, 1959.

———. *Nature and Culture: Ethical Thought in the French Enlightenment.* Baltimore, 1963.

Cross, Barbara M. *Horace Bushnell: Minister to a Changing America.* Chicago, 1958.

Cross, Whitney. *The Burned-Over District: The Social and Intellectual History of Enthusiastic Religion in Western New York, 1800–1850.* Ithaca, New York, 1950.

Curti, Merle. "The Great Mr. Locke, America's Philosopher, 1783–1861," Huntington Library, *Bulletin,* number 11 (1937), 107–51.

———. "Human Nature in American Thought: The Age of Reason and Morality, 1750–1860," *Political Science Quarterly,* 68 (1953), 354–75.

———. *The Social Ideas of American Educators.* Patterson, New Jersey, 1959. First published, 1935.

Davie, George Elder. *The Democratic Intellect: Scotland and Her Universities in the Nineteenth Century.* Edinburgh, 1961.

Davis, David B. *The Problem of Slavery in Western Culture.* Ithaca, New York, 1966.

Davis, Merrell R. "Emerson's 'Reason' and the Scottish Philosophers," *New England Quarterly,* 17 (1944), 209–28.

Delmage, Rutherford E. "The American Idea of Progress, 1750–1800," American Philosophical Society, *Proceedings,* 91 (1947), 307–14.

Denison, John Hopkins. *Mark Hopkins: A Biography.* New York, 1935.

Dewey, John. "From Absolutism to Experimentalism," *Contemporary American Philosophy: Personal Statements,* George P. Adams and William P. Montague, ed. Two volumes. New York, 1930, II, 13–27.

Dorfman, Joseph. *The Economic Mind in American Civilization, 1606–1865.* Two volumes. New York, 1946.

Eby, Louise Saxe. *The Quest for Moral Law*. New York, 1944.

Ekirch, Arthur E. *The Idea of Progress in America, 1815–1860*. New York, 1944.

Elkins, Stanley M. *Slavery: A Problem in American Institutional and Intellectual Life*. Chicago, 1959.

Elsbree, Oliver Wendell. "Samuel Hopkins and His Doctrine of Benevolence," *New England Qaurterly*, 8 (1935), 535–50.

Fay, Jay Wharton. *American Psychology before William James*. New York, 1930.

Fiering, Norman S. "President Samuel Johnson and the Circle of Knowledge," *William and Mary Quarterly*, 28, ser. 3 (1971), 199–236.

———. "Moral Philosophy in America, 1650–1750, and Its British Context." Unpublished doctoral dissertation, Columbia University, 1969.

Fletcher, Robert S. *A History of Oberlin College from Its Foundation through the Civil War*. Two volumes. Oberlin, 1943.

Flew, Robert N. *The Idea of Perfection in Christian Theology: An Historical Study of the Christian Ideal for a Perfect Life*. London, 1934.

Foner, Eric. *Free Soil, Free Labor, Free Men: The Ideology of the Republican Party before the Civil War*. New York, London, Oxford, 1970.

Foster, Charles I. *An Errand of Mercy: The Evangelical United Front, 1790–1870*. Chapel Hill, 1960.

Foster, Frank Hugh. *A Genetic History of the New England Theology*. Chicago, 1907.

Fox, Dixon Ryan. "The Protestant Counter-Reformation in America," *New York History*, 16 (1935), 19–35.

Frederickson, George M. *The Inner Civil War: Northern Intellectuals and the Crisis of the Union*. New York, 1965.

Frothingham, Octavius Brooks. *Boston Unitarianism, 1820–1850*. New York, 1890.

———. *Recollections and Impressions, 1822–1890*. New York, 1891.

Gabriel, Ralph Henry. *Course of American Democratic Thought*. New York, 1940.

———. *Religion and Learning at Yale: The Church of Christ in the College and University, 1757–1957*. New Haven, 1958.

Gay, Peter. *The Enlightenment: An Interpretation*. Two volumes. New York, 1966, 1968.

Gillispie, Charles C. *The Edge of Objectivity: An Essay in the History of Scientific Ideas.* Princeton, New Jersey, 1960.

Glick, Wendell. "Bishop [*sic*] Paley in America," *New England Quarterly*, 27 (1954), 347–54.

Grave, S. A. *The Scottish Philosophy of Common Sense.* Oxford, 1960.

Green, Martin. *The Problem of Boston: Some Readings in Cultural History.* New York, 1966.

Greene, Evarts B. "A Puritan Counter-Reformation," American Antiquarian Society, *Proceedings*, ser. 2nd., 42 (1932), 17–46.

Greene, John C. *Darwin and the Modern World-View.* Baton Rouge, 1961.

———. *The Death of Adam: Evolution and Its Impact on Western Thought.* Ames, Iowa, 1959.

Griffin, Clifford S. "Religious Benevolence as Social Control, 1835–1860," *Mississippi Valley Historical Review*, 44 (1957), 423–44.

———. *Their Brothers' Keepers: Moral Stewardship in the United States, 1800–1865.* New Brunswick, New Jersey, 1960.

Gusfield, Joseph R. *Symbolic Crusade: Status Politics and the American Temperance Movement.* Urbana, Illinois, 1963.

Guttmann, Allen. *The Conservative Tradition in America.* New York, 1967.

Haddow, Anna. *Political Science in American Colleges and Universities, 1636–1900.* New York, 1939.

Halévy, Elie. *England in 1815.* E. I. Watkin and D. A. Barker, tr. Revised edition, London, 1949. First published in French, 1913.

Hall, G. Stanley. "On the History of American College Text-Books and Teaching in Logic, Ethics, Psychology and Allied Subjects," American Antiquarian Society, *Proceedings*, 9, ser. 2 (1894), 137–74.

———. "Philosophy in the United States," *Mind*, 4 (1879), 89–105.

Handy, Robert T. "The Protestant Quest for a Christian America, 1830–1930," *Church History*, 23 (1953), 8–20.

Haroutunian, Joseph. *Piety versus Moralism: The Passing of the New England Theology.* New York, 1932.

Hawkins, Richard L. *Auguste Comte and the United States, 1816–1853.* Cambridge, Massachusetts, 1936.

Heimert, Alan. *Religion and the American Mind: From the Great Awakening to the Revolution.* Cambridge, Massachusetts, 1966.

Higham, John. "Beyond Consensus: The Historian as Moral Critic," *American Historical Review*, 67 (1962), 609–25.

———. *From Boundlessness to Consolidation: The Transformation of American Culture.* Ann Arbor, 1969.

Himmelfarb, Gertrude. *Darwin and the Darwinian Revolution.* New York, 1968. First edition, 1959.

———. *Victorian Minds.* New York, 1968.

Hofstadter, Richard. *Academic Freedom in the Age of the College.* New York, 1955.

———. *Anti-Intellectualism in American Life.* New York, 1962.

Hofstadter, Richard and C. DeWitt Hardy. *The Development and Scope of Higher Education in the United States.* New York, 1962.

Hopkins, Charles H. *The Rise of the Social Gospel in American Protestantism, 1865–1915.* New Haven, 1940.

Houghton, Walter E. *The Victorian Frame of Mind, 1830–1870.* New Haven, 1957.

Howe, Daniel W. *The Unitarian Conscience: Harvard Moral Philosophy, 1806–1861.* Cambridge, Massachusetts, 1970.

Hudson, Winthrop. *The Great Tradition of the American Churches.* New York, 1953.

James, Walker T. "The Philosophy of Noah Porter (1811–1892)." Unpublished doctoral dissertation, Columbia University.

Jessop, Thomas Temund. *A Bibliography of David Hume and of Scottish Philosophy from Francis Hutcheson to Lord Balfour.* London, 1938.

Jones, Olin McKendree. *Empiricism and Intuitionism in Reid's Common Sense Philosophy.* Princeton, 1927.

Kelley, Robert. *The Transatlantic Persuasion: The Liberal-Democratic Mind in the Age of Gladstone.* New York, 1969.

Kolesnik, Walter B. *Mental Discipline in Modern Education.* Madison, 1958.

Kwiat, Joseph J. "Thoreau's Philosophical Apprenticeship," *New England Quarterly*, 18 (1945), 51–69.

Laurie, Henry. *The Scottish Philosophy in Its National Development.* Glasgow, 1902.

LeDuc, Thomas. *Piety and Intellect at Amherst College, 1865–1912.* New York, 1946.

Lehman, Paul L. *Ethics in a Christian Context.* London, 1963.
Lewis, C. S. *De Descriptione Temporum.* Cambridge, England, 1955.
Lindström, Harold Gastaf Ake. *Wesley and Sanctification: A Study in the Doctrine of Salvation.* Stockholm, 1946.
Lippmann, Walter. *Essays in the Public Philosophy.* Boston, 1955.
————. *A Preface to Morals.* New York, 1929.
Lipset, Seymour Martin. *The First New Nation.* New York, 1963.
Lukacs, John. *The Passing of the Modern Age.* New York, Evanston, London, 1970.
MacIntyre, Alasdair and Paul Ricoeur. *The Religious Significance of Atheism.* New York and London, 1969.
MacIntyre, Alasdair. *Secularization and Moral Change.* London, 1967.
McLachlan, James. *American Boarding Schools: A Historical Study.* New York, 1970.
MacLoughlin, William G. *The Meaning of Henry Ward Beecher: An Essay on the Shifting Values of Mid-Victorian America, 1840–1870.* New York, 1970.
Madden, Edward H. *Civil Disobedience and Moral Law in Nineteenth-Century American Philosophy.* Seattle and London, 1968.
————. "Francis Wayland and the Limits of Moral Responsibility," American Philosophical Society, *Proceedings*, 106 (1962), 348–59.
Madden, William A. "The Victorian Sensibility," *Victorian Studies*, 7 (1963), 67–97.
Martin, Terence. *The Instructed Vision: Scottish Common Sense Philosophy and the Origins of American Fiction.* Bloomington, Indiana, 1961.
Maslow, Abraham (ed.). *New Knowledge in Human Values.* New York, 1959.
Mathews, Donald G. *Slavery and Methodism: A Chapter in American Morality, 1780–1845.* Princeton, 1965.
May, Henry F. *The End of American Innocence: A Study of the First Years of Our Own Time, 1912–1917.* New York, 1959.
————. *The Protestant Churches and Industrial America.* New York, 1963. First published in 1949.
Mead, Sidney E. *The Lively Experiment: The Shaping of Christianity in America.* New York, 1963.

Mead, Sidney E. *William Nathaniel Taylor, 1786–1858: A Connecticut Liberal.* Chicago, 1942.

Merideth, Robert. *The Politics of the Universe: Edward Beecher, Abolition and Orthodoxy.* Nashville, 1963.

Miller, Perry. *The Life of the Mind in America from the Revolution to the Civil War.* New York, 1965.

Murray, James O. *Francis Wayland.* Boston and New York, 1891.

Niebuhr, H. Richard. *Christ and Culture.* New York, 1951.

———. *The Kingdom of God in America.* New York, 1937.

Niebuhr, Reinhold. *The Children of Light and the Children of Darkness.* New York, 1944.

———. *The Irony of American History.* New York, 1952.

———. *Moral Man and Immoral Society: A Study in Ethics and Politics.* New York, 1932.

Nye, Russel Blaine. *The Cultural Life in the New Nation, 1776–1830.* New York, 1960.

Nygren, Anders. *Agape and Eros: A Study of the Christian Idea of Love.* A. G. Herbert, tr. New York, 1939.

O'Connor, Michael J. L. *Origins of Academic Economics in the United States.* New York, 1944.

Palmer, Paul A. "Benthamism in England and America," *American Political Science Review,* 35 (1941), 855–71.

Passmore, John. "Darwin's Impact on British Metaphysics," *Victorian Studies,* 3 (1959), 41–54.

———. *The Perfectability of Man.* New York, 1970.

Perry, Ralph Barton. *Characteristically American.* New York, 1949.

———. *General Theory of Value.* New York, 1926.

Persons, Stow. *American Minds: A History of Ideas.* New York, 1958.

——— (ed.). *Evolutionary Thought in America.* New Haven, 1950.

Peterson, George F. *The New England College in the Age of the University.* Amherst, Massachusetts, 1964.

Pettit, Norman. *The Heart Prepared: Grace and Conversion in Puritan Spiritual Life.* New Haven and London, 1966.

Pingel, Martha M. *An American Utilitarian: Richard Hildreth as a Philosopher.* New York, 1948.

Post, Albert. *Popular Freethought in America, 1825–1850.* New York, 1943.

Rand, Benjamin. "Philosophical Instruction at Harvard University, from 1636 to 1906," *Harvard Graduates' Magazine*, 37 (1928), 29–47, 188–200.

Randall, John Herman, Jr. "The Changing Impact of Darwin on Philosophy," *Journal of the History of Ideas*, 22 (1961), 435–62.

Raphael, David Daiches. "Bishop Butler's View of Conscience," *Philosophy*, 24 (1949), 219–38.

———. *The Moral Sense*. London, 1947.

Riley, I. Woodbridge. *American Philosophy: The Early Schools*. New York, 1907.

Roback, A. A. *History of American Psychology*. New York, 1952.

Rudolph, Frederick. *Mark Hopkins and the Log: Williams College, 1836–1872*. New Haven, Connecticut, 1956.

———. *The American College and University*. New York, 1962.

Salisbury, E. G. *In the Days of Mark Hopkins: Story of Williams College*. Phelps, New York, 1927.

Sanford, Charles L. *Quest for Paradise: Europe and the American Moral Imagination*. Urbana, Illinois, 1961.

Santayana, George. *Character and Opinion in the United States*. New York, 1920.

———. *Winds of Doctrine and Platonism and the Spiritual Life*. New York, 1957.

Schmidt, George P. "Intellectual Crosscurrents in American Colleges, 1825–1855," *American Historical Review*, 42 (1935), 46–67.

———. *The Liberal Arts College: A Chapter in American Cultural History*. New Brunswick, New Jersey, 1957.

———. *The Old Time College President*. New York, 1930.

Schneewind, Jerome B. "Moral Problems and Moral Philosophy in the Victorian Period," *Victorian Studies*, 9, supplement (1965), 29–46.

Schneider, Herbert W. *A History of American Philosophy*. New York, 1946.

Segerstedt, Torngy T. *The Problem of Knowledge in Scottish Philosophy*. Lund, 1935.

Seth, Andrew. *Scottish Philosophy: A Comparison of the Scottish and German Answers to Hume*. Edinburgh and London, 1885.

Sloan, Douglas. *The Scottish Enlightenment and the American College Ideal*. New York, 1971.

Smith, Timothy L. *Revivalism and Social Reform in Mid-Nineteenth-Century America.* New York and Nashville, 1957.

Smith, Wilson. "Francis Lieber's Moral Philosophy," *Huntington Library Quarterly*, 17 (1955), 395–408.

———. *Professors and Public Ethics: Studies of Northern Moral Philosophers before the Civil War.* Ithaca, New York, 1956.

———. "William Paley's Theological Utilitarianism in America," *William and Mary Quarterly*, ser. 3rd. 11 (1954), 402–34.

Snow, Louis Franklin. *The College Curriculum in the United States.* New York, 1907.

Sproat, John G. *"The Best Men": Liberal Reformers in the Gilded Age.* New York, 1968.

Stephen, Leslie. *History of English Thought in the Eighteenth Century.* Two volumes. Third edition; London, 1902.

Stephenson, George M. *The Puritan Heritage.* New York, 1952.

Suter, Rufus. "The Concept of Morality in the Philosophy of Jonathan Edwards," *Journal of Religion*, 14 (1934), 265–72.

Sweet, William Warren. *Religion in the Development of American Culture, 1765–1840.* New York, 1952.

Sykes, Hugh and Watson, George (ed.). *The English Mind: Studies in the English Moralists Presented to Basil Willey.* Cambridge, 1964.

Tewksbury, Donald G. *The Founding of American Colleges and Universities before the Civil War with Particular Reference to the Religious Influences Bearing upon the College Movement.* New York, 1932.

Tholfsen, Trygve R. "Intellectual Origins of Mid-Victorian Stability," *Political Science Quarterly*, 86 (1971), 57–91.

Thomas, John L. "Romantic Reform in America, 1815–1865," *American Quarterly*, 17 (1965), 658–81.

Thompson, Cameron. "John Locke and New England Transcendentalism," *New England Quarterly*, 35 (1962), 435–57.

Todd, Edgeley Woodman. "Philosophical Ideas at Harvard College, 1817–1837," *New England Quarterly*, 16 (1943), 63–90.

Tomsich, John. *A Genteel Endeavor: American Culture and Politics in the Gilded Age.* Stanford, California. 1971.

Tuveson, Ernest Lee. *The Imagination as a Means of Grace: Locke and the Aesthetics of Romanticism.* Berkeley and Los Angeles, 1960.

——. "The Origins of the 'Moral Sense,'" *Huntington Library Quarterly,* 11 (1948), 241–59.

——. *Redeemer Nation: The Idea of America's Millennial Role.* Chicago and London, 1968.

Tyack, David. "Forming the National Character," *Harvard Educational Review,* 36 (1966), 29–41.

Tyler, Alice Felt. *Freedom's Ferment: Phases of American Social History from the Colonial Period to the Outbreak of the Civil War.* Minneapolis, 1944.

VanDeusen, Glyndon G. "Some Aspects of Whig Thought and Theory in the Jacksonian Period," *American Historical Review,* 63 (1958), 305–22.

Veysey, Laurence R. *The Emergence of the American University.* Chicago and London, 1965.

Voitle, Robert. "The Reason of the English Enlightenment," *Studies on Voltaire and the Eighteenth Century,* 27 (1963), 1735–74.

Warren, Austin. *The New England Conscience.* Ann Arbor, 1966.

Welter, Rush. *Popular Education and Democratic Thought in America.* New York and London, 1962.

White, Morton. *Social Thought in America: The Revolt against Formalism.* Boston, 1957. First published, 1947.

Wiebe, Robert H. *The Search for Order, 1877–1920.* New York, 1967.

Willey, Basil. *The English Moralists.* London, 1964.

Williams, Daniel Day. *The Andover Liberals: A Study in American Theology.* New York, 1941.

Williams, George H. (ed.). *The Harvard Divinity School: Its Place in Harvard University and in American Culture.* Boston, 1954.

Williams, Raymond. *Culture and Society, 1780–1950.* New York, 1958.

Wilson, Raymond Jackson. *In Quest of Community: Social Philosophy in the United States, 1860–1920.* London, Oxford, New York, 1968.

Wood, Herbert George. *Belief and Unbelief since 1850.* Cambridge, England, 1955.

Bibliography

Wright, Benjamin Fletcher, Jr. *American Interpretations of Natural Law: A Study in the History of Political Thought.* Cambridge, Massachusetts, 1931.

Wright, Walter E. C. "Oberlin's Contribution to Ethics," *Bibliotheca Sacra*, 57 (1900), 429–44.

Index

Academic moralists: Enlightenment legacy of, 10, 129; influence of, 125–26, 135–36, 141–45; mission of, 4–5, 6, 125; and party politics, 114–15; public role of, 131; theories of society, 112–13, 129; values of, 28–30, 129; view of moral obligation, 74–75; and virtue, 99–107. *See also* Moral philosophy; Textbooks

Adams, Henry, 125

Adams, Jasper: on Christian duties, 71, 72–73; life and philosophy, 147–48; practical emphasis, 26, 58–59

Adrian College: Asa Mahan at, 152

Agency, moral. *See* Will

Alexander, Archibald: defends Calvinism, 58; and ethical theory, 21, 160; on free will, 55–57; life and philosophy, 20–22, 148; mentioned, 49, 93

Alger, Horatio, 142

Amherst: Joseph Haven at, 150

Analogical technique, 24–25, 44–45

Andover Theological Seminary, 13, 123–24

Arminianism, 20, 25

Associationist theory of mind, 158

Associations, voluntary, 115

Astronomy: analogy with moral philosophy, 4–5

Atonement theory, 91–92

Augustine, Saint, 14

Baccalaureate sermons, 151

Bacon, Francis, 54, 106

Bailey, Silas: on Francis Wayland, 134–35

Baird, Robert: on atonement, 91; on free will, 58

Bascom, John, 128

Beattie, James, 37, 39–40

Beecher, Henry Ward, 25

Bellamy, Edward, 99, 119

Bellamy, Joseph, 91

Benevolence, disinterested: Charles G. Finney on, 150; Mark Hopkins on, 159; Francis Hutcheson on, 36–37; pleasures of, 100–101; and virtue, 77–82; Francis Wayland on, 72–73, 100–101

Bentham, Jeremy, 22, 158

Bowen, Francis: as critic of Wayland, 15; and economic order, 102; and ethical theory, 160; on harmony of interests, 103; life and philosophy, 17–20, 148; on moral government, 95–97; on political economy, 104; and Scottish common-sense philos-